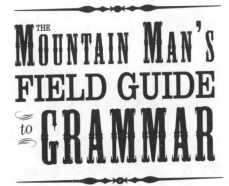

# THE MOUNTAIN MAN'S FIELD GUIDE to GRAMMAR

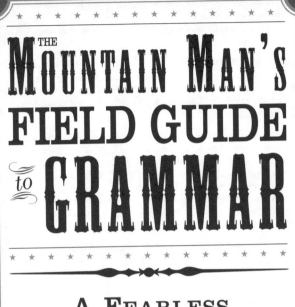

# THE MOUNTAIN MAN'S FIELD GUIDE to GRAMMAR

## A FEARLESS ADVENTURE IN GRAMMAR, STYLE, AND USAGE

SOURCEBOOKS, INC.®
NAPERVILLE, ILLINOIS

GARY SPINA

Published by Sourcebooks, Inc.
P.O. Box 4410, Naperville, Illinois   60567–4410
(630) 961–3900
Fax: (630) 961–2168
www.sourcebooks.com

Library of Congress Cataloging-in-Publication Data
Spina, Gary.
  The mountain man's field guide to grammar : a fearless adventure in
grammar, style, and usage / Gary Spina.
     p. cm.
  Includes bibliographical references.
  ISBN-13: 978-1-4022-0740-2
  ISBN-10: 1-4022-0740-9
  1.   English language—Grammar—Handbooks, manuals, etc. 2.
English language—Rhetoric—Handbooks, manuals, etc. 3. English
language—Usage—Handbooks, manuals, etc. I. Title.

PE1112.S68 2006
428.2—dc22
                                                    2006003649

Printed and bound in India by Imago
         IM   10   9   8   7   6   5   4

# DEDICATION

---

This book is for Bob Fleming and John Spina, two adventurers, two tramps in their younger days, two men of character, honor, and courage. Their passion is the woods and trout streams and the vast mountain wilderness of the far northwest. They love boats and cabins, wolves and hawks, and the wine country, which is anywhere they are. This book is for them and the good memories and the good times back when old Bob and young John caught some fair-sized salmon on Alaska's Resurrection Bay. Few people will ever see the wild and experience it as they have.

# CONTENTS

# Acknowledgments

My editor and friend Carrie Obry believed in this project from the very beginning. It was Carrie's genius, vision, and professionalism that turned a disorganized manuscript into a book. As the project advanced, Bethany Brown, Rachel Jay, and Ewurama Ewusi-Mensah edited out most of my mistakes and succeeded in making me look smart.

Before anyone else, it was Dianne Hermann who was the first to believe this grand foolishness was worthy enough to be published. Through several revisions, two or three restructurings, and countless, tedious proofreading, Dianne would work late into the night reading every word. She poured over each page of the manuscript with youthful laughter, unwavering encouragement, and sage advice. She was ever at my side, ever looking over my shoulder, ever at the ready with marginal patience and an occasional back-of-the-head slap of admonishment.

It was I alone, of course, who insisted on leaving some random blunders and outright stupidity within the pages of this book so as not to disappoint those readers who delight in pointing them out at book signings and dinner parties and such.

# Introduction

As a schoolboy, I didn't see any value in education because I knew even then, when I grew up, I was going to be a mountain man. I was going to be a free trapper, as distinguished from a trapper who signed on with and worked for a fur company. It didn't matter to me that the last old mountain man had bundled up his plews a hundred years before.

"Mountain men don't need no education," I assured myself. I figured that out all by myself. Alas, man is ever-cursed with the dreams he holds dear, further cursed with the fact that he usually gets exactly what he asks for in life. When I actually began to roam the woods and mountains and write it all down, I discovered a man needs grammar as much as he needs the love and warmth of the right woman on a cold, wintry night.

But real American stories require genuine American usage and grammar. Back in the merry old land across the pond, they tell a story of Winston Churchill and Lady Astor. The two could not suffer each other's company. Each found the other an intolerable abomination—politically, socially, and genetically. One evening at a dinner party, a particularly devilish hostess thought she'd have some fun by seating the old bulldog and the prissy lady across from each other at the table.

Not long into the meal, an exasperated Lady Astor was heard to remark, "Honestly, Mr. Churchill, if you were my husband, I would poison your tea."

With no stomach to ponder the prospect of marriage to the lady, Churchill rasped out, "Madam, if I were your husband, I should drink it."

The story always fascinated me because Churchill used the word *should* when any self-respecting American would have used *would*. The truth be told, there is a vast Atlantic ocean of difference between the English language and the American language. And after our bloody Revolution and that unpleasantness of 1812 through early 1815, we've earned the right to our own language and grammar—and political correctness be damned.

Throughout the history of America, the American language has heralded our freedom, our concepts, our fundamental articulation of justice, fairness, and morality. Words constitute our laws, our understanding of ourselves and our world. It may be true that the American language is alive and ever-changing, yet words still mean. Words still convey ideas, moods, emotions. How does one standardize an ever-evolving linguistic life force so that it remains true enough and precise enough to bind wedding vows, contracts, handshakes, treaties, and our precious Constitution?

Precise grammar requires logic and a bit of intuitive deduction. The old America and its clarity of thought and language are gone. Gone are the old mountain men who lived by their word and relied upon their wits. Gone are the free, wild Indians and the warriors, their faces painted black, who staked themselves out to die in battle for honor and glory. This book mourns their loss and celebrates their memory as it makes a humble effort to restore some logic and precision to our American language.

In writing this book, I have attempted to make each line of text, each rule of grammar, and each example fresh and new and original. But a noun is a noun and a verbal is a verbal, and festooning them in gaudy finery can neither add nor detract from their essence. American grammar and construction—the essential stuff—is staid and stately, elegant, sensuous, raw, and beautiful.

Gary Spina
Northern Cheyenne Indian Reservation
Rosebud County, Montana

# PREFACE:

## The Mountain Man

*"There's a race of men that don't fit in."*

— ROBERT W. SERVICE

The history of the mountain man enjoys a mixed review. Some mountain men, like Jedediah Smith, were well read and highly educated. Others, like Jim Bridger, could not write their own name. Some were murderers and thieves; others were men of honor and probity. All were adventurers. All were renegades from the safety, comfort, and restrictions of society.

The truth is, the mountain man was many things loathsome and many things laudable. He was a man of action, vision, and purpose. He was a shiftless, aimless wanderer. He lived by the measure of his manhood, by his wits and his courage, and by his word. Some mountain men were cowardly dolts who cheated and lied and couldn't be trusted with another man's wife, whiskey, horse, or rifle. But the mountain man opened up the vast American wilderness and led the way west. And maybe he did it all in spite of himself.

Neither the mountain men, nor the Indian of old would be impressed by the more than 500,000 words in the modern English language. Across the vast prairies, and in the wild Rockies, deeds spoke volumes. "It does not require many words to speak the truth," said Chief Joseph of the Nez Perce.

Mountain men were known to husband their words. Words a mountain man didn't know were overcome by the words he could make up—"possibles" being a good example. A "possible sack," or simply "possibles," was a rucksack or backpack to hold all the emergency gear and possible necessities a mountain man might need in the wild. It was foolish to take so much gear into the mountains that you needed a horse to carry it all. Horses and the gear on their backs were routinely stolen by Indians or opportunistic white men of less than sterling character. A mountain man carried all he ever needed in his possible sack.

Winfred Blevins, in his book *Give Your Heart to the Hawks*, does an excellent job of explaining some of the mountain man jargon. When you read Blevins it's as though you are back in early America sitting across a campfire listening to an old trapper spinning his yarns. I have Winfred Blevins to thank for getting me back up to speed on most of my mountain man terms, and for teaching me a few new ones.

"Diggin's" usually referred to white man's houses and life in town. Mountain men eschewed streets and houses and public buildings. A mountain man would sooner "go under" (die) in "them thar mountains yonder" than live safe and soft in white man's diggin's. "Dupont" was gunpowder, so named for the manufacturer. Tobacco was "bacca," which at times sold or traded for a plew a plug.

The word "plew" originates from the French *pelu* meaning hairy or having hair. A plew was a fur-bearing skin, especially of the beaver, particularly one of prime quality. In the heyday of the old trappers, beaver skins sold for as high as ten dollars a plew in St. Louis.

"Some" was said of a person or thing held in the highest esteem. "Kit Carson—he was some, all right."

"Wagh!" is another mountain man word, somewhat more difficult to define. It is a guttural exclamation of amazement or affirmation, as in: "Wagh! That squaw was some, you betcha!" Or maybe that Indian gal had a taste for fancy trimmings, trinkets, or highfalutin amenities a mountain man called "foofaraw." Foofaraw had a connotation, if not denotation, of phony, high-toned ways, so a gal—Indian or white— with a bit of the foofaraw in her was repugnant to a mountain man.

"Castoreum" is secretion from the scrotum of the beaver. It could be used as a medicinal salve to ease the pain of a wound and to "draw out" swelling. It was also the "medicine" the trapper used to lure the beaver to his trap. Some trappers called it castor or castorum.

When a mountain man would brag about his rifle (and in effect about himself), he might say, "She shoots center."

A real mountain man had the "ha'r of the b'ar" in him. He knew "the way the stick floats." He could tell a tall tale shamelessly, or tell the truth if you cornered him into it. He knew that effective communication doesn't take a lot of words, just good ones.

# THE HORSE BEFORE THE TRAVOIS:

## Parts of Speech and the Basic Sentence

*"Bein' ready fer trouble keeps trouble at a distance."*

⟨SILAS POTTER⟩

On the shingle of the gray mountain creek, the big man stripped off his elkskin shirt and britches. Naked except for his moccasins, the man stepped into the icy water and waded upstream. The cold autumn breeze blew the last of the mist across the water and into the trees along the creek bank. The morning sun shone through the mist. The sun was climbing higher in the sky, ever-stronger, ever-warmer.

The naked man in the creek was Big Jake McLaughlin. Big Jake was a mountain man and trapper. Other men said many things about Big Jake, some of them true. But men who knew him agreed: Big Jake was a man totally without fear.

Every mountain man, trapper, scout, and guide who knew him, knew Big Jake was fearless, dumb, and lucky, attended by an inordinate charm that had kept him alive where other men had lost their scalps. The Indian, too, who crossed his path knew it. There were scars across Big Jake's face from a grizzly attack years before. There were scars on his chest and back from encounters with hostile Indians and drunken, jealous husbands. His big hands were gnarly, and he walked with a crippled, lumbering limp. But there was a calm serenity in the big man's eyes. Big Jake had struck a balance, and here in the mountains, living life was a simple proposition.

Big Jake waded upstream in the frigid creek, as casual as a man in a summer pool. The creek was cold and gray and fast, but walking in the water would hide his scent and his tracks. His dark eyes scanned the bank for signs of the beaver he knew were there. At a beaver slide, Big Jake smiled. There along the bank were the obvious markings of the critters at play.

Big Jake waded closer to the edge of the bank. He took a trap from his sack, spread the steel jaws, set the trigger in place, and carefully placed it underwater on the squishy creek-bed. Overhead, above the treetops, the puffy white clouds blew softly and steadily across the high blue sky...

* * *

First things first. Before we even begin, the gentle reader needs to know a few things. For the purposes of instruction, we shall, at times, refer to the reader as "crittur." It is a term of quasi-endearment among us mountain men types. There were other names mountain men used in addressing one another: "coon" and "hoss" and "child" and others better left untold.

The first thing a crittur needs to understand is the Parts of Speech. There are eight of them. The eight parts of speech constitute the skeleton of American grammar. From this skeleton, all grammar and usage are fleshed out.

## Parts of Speech:

**Noun:** A noun is a word that names a person, place, thing, or idea.

Because *modesty* was a *notion* foreign to most *mountain men*, *Stinky Petey* thought nothing of scratching the *seat* of his *britches* in *church*.

**Pronoun:** A pronoun is a word that takes the place of a noun.

*He* thought *it* a natural thing to scratch wherever *he* itched.

**Verb:** A verb is a word that shows action or a state of being.

Sometimes he *scratched* so hard,
he *would* actually *shed* a tear
and *smile* at the same time.
Stinky Petey, of course, *was*
unaware of his faux pas.

**Adjective:** An adjective is a word that describes a noun or pronoun.

It all felt *good*, and Stinky Petey
never noticed the stares of the
*disgusted* congregation.

**Adverb:** An adverb is a word that modifies a verb, an adjective, or another adverb.

The creek water ran *very fast* and
*numbingly cold*. Stinky Petey
carried one *very* old bar of soap.

**Conjunction:** A conjunction is a word that links words or groups of words in a sentence.

He knew he should bathe, *but*
he was afraid of water *and*
distrustful of soap.

**Preposition:** A preposition is a word that relates a noun or pronoun to other words in a sentence.

*Of* all the men *in* camp, Stinky Petey alone was unconcerned *about* hygiene.

**Interjection:** An interjection is a word that expresses shock or strong emotion.

"*Phew*!" was usually the first word out of the mouths of folks who met Stinky Petey. When he got down wind of Dirty Doris, he shouted, "*Eureka*!" at finally meeting a woman who could understand him.

## Other Grammar Elements:

In addition to the parts of speech, you will need to understand the following terms:

**Direct object:** A direct object is a noun or pronoun (usually) that receives the action directly from the action verb. A direct object answers the question whom? or what?

Dirty Doris spit tobacco *juice*.

**Transitive verb:** A transitive verb is an action verb that takes a direct object.

She *kept* a pet skunk.

**Indirect object:** An indirect object is a noun or pronoun (usually) that indirectly receives the action of a transitive verb. Remember, when I say transitive verb, it means you already have a direct object in place. You cannot have an indirect object if you do not first have a direct object. An indirect object answers the question to whom? for whom? to what? or for what?

She gave *Stinky Petey* all her kisses.

**Intransitive verb:** An intransitive verb is a verb that does not take a direct object.

But she only *slept* with wet dogs.

**Article:** An article is a special adjective. There are only three articles: *a, an,* and *the*.

Watching *the* romance blossom between Stinky Petey and Dirty Doris was both *a* hoot and *an* abomination.

## Verbals (Gerund, Infinitive, Participle):

**Gerund:** A gerund is a present tense verb with *ing* as a suffix. Once you add the *ing*, the verb becomes a verbal noun, performing almost all the functions of a noun.

*Tracking* is a spiritual endeavor to those who do it right.

**Infinitive:** An infinitive is a basic verb form preceded by the word *to*. Infinitives and infinitive phrases serve as nouns, adjectives, and adverbs.

*To follow* the tracks of a man or animal, a tracker must understand the spirit of that man or animal.

**Participle:** Add the suffix *ing* to verbs to form present participles. Add the suffix *ed* to most verbs to form past participles. A participle can serve as a verb or an adjective.

The trapper *wading* in the creek is Big Jake.
The *harried* stranger came into camp looking for food.

## THE SENTENCE: HOW IT'S DONE

The second first thing a crittur needs to understand is the sentence. A sentence is a complete thought expressed plainly, cleanly, and logically. All sentences fall within four basic types, although some below are "clipped" sentences, which we will discuss later.

A declarative sentence makes a statement or pronouncement. It is punctuated by a period.

> Big Jake is a liar.
> No, Big Jake's not a liar. He's a horse thief, maybe, but not a liar.
> Well, either way, somebody ought to hang him.

An imperative sentence makes a request or gives a command. It, too, is punctuated by a period. In imperative sentences, the subject *you* is often implied, so that the following can be a complete sentence:

> Go. (Meaning: You, go. Or: You, go away.)
> Go git a rope. (Or, if a crittur is speaking excitedly: Go git a rope!)

An interrogative sentence asks a question. It is punctuated by a question mark.

> Don't we need to give him a trial first?
> What fer? (Or, if a crittur is speaking excitedly: What fer!)

An exclamatory sentence expresses shock, surprise, or strong emotion. It is punctuated by an exclamation mark.

> He could be innocent!
> No way!

The grammatical laws of the sentence can get downright lawless when emotions are running high. What is normally a respectable interrogative sentence may actually be an exclamatory sentence when the question is rhetorical and expresses shock, wonder, or strong emotion. (*What!*) (*You're kidding!*) An imperative sentence may be exclamatory when the command or request is urgent or expresses excitement or strong emotion. (*Get me out of here!*) A declarative sentence is also an exclamatory sentence when it emanates from surprise or strong emotion. (*That's a lie!*)

### *Writing a Complete Sentence*
A sentence is a group of words that expresses a complete thought and has a subject and predicate. A complete sentence needs two elements:

1. **The Subject:** a person, place, thing, or idea
   Subject = NOUN or PRONOUN
2. **The Predicate:** what that person, place, thing, or idea is, or what he, she, or it is doing, feeling, or experiencing.
   Predicate = VERB

Each of the two elements (subject and predicate) must be clearly defined so the reader or listener will not be confused, misled, or misinformed.

Charlie traps in the high mountains.

**Subject**          **Predicate**
Charlie              traps in the high mountains.

When we break a sentence down into its simple subject and simple predicate, we sharpen our focus. Other sentence elements flesh in the rest.

The mountains can sustain a wise man or kill a fool.

**Simple Subject**   **Simple Predicate**
mountains (noun)     can sustain (verb) can kill (verb)

*Subject Nouns and Pronouns*
That summer at rendezvous, Big Jake went searching through the encampment looking to quench a powerful thirst. The subject of his search was some hooch. It was there he first met Iron Skillet, also searching the encampment. The subject of her search was some hoochie-koochie.

That night Big Jake got himself hooched up, all right. The next morning he found himself sentenced to painful years of grief with a ferocious, evil-eyed hellcat who was now his wife. The big guy may have avoided all that had he understood subjects and sentences beforehand.

The subject of a sentence is usually a noun or pronoun. Note below that ideas (such as *courage* and *honor*) are nouns. Note the pronoun alternatives:

| Noun (person, place, thing, idea) | Pronoun (taking the place of a noun) |
| --- | --- |
| horse | it |
| girl | she |
| Tom | he |
| Tom and Henry | they |
| courage | it |
| honor | it |
| Tom's | his |
| Tom and Henry's | theirs (owned by both) |
| Tom's and Henry's | theirs (owned individually) |

*The Predicate*

The predicate of a sentence is always a verb. Note below that thought processes (such as *think* and *worry*) are action verbs. The "be" verbs express a state of existence.

| Action Verbs | "Be" Verbs |
| --- | --- |
| run | am |
| jump | is |
| swim | are |
| talk | was |
| think | were |
| worry | be, been, being |

None of the other mountain men ever knew his last name, or ever cared. To them he was simply Stinky Petey. The Paiute called him Down Wind Man, the Crow and Cheyenne called him Dog Breath. But the Sioux probably had it the most accurate. The Sioux called him Wet Dog Rolls in Buffalo Dung.

Stinky Petey was a decent enough fellow as long as you kept a careful eye on him around your valuables, and as long as you didn't take everything he said as gospel truth, and as long as he had nothing to gain by your sudden demise, and as long as he stayed sober. But Big Jake liked Stinky Petey most of the time because Stinky Petey was consistent and because Stinky Petey never pretended to be anything he wasn't. Big Jake figured that was more than could be said for most mountain men.

## THE FOUR BASIC ELEMENTS OF A SENTENCE

We have looked at the two elements basic to a sentence: the subject and the predicate. But the predicate itself may contain two distinct elements—for a total of four elements—that need understanding. We need to understand:

1. Subject
2. Predicate
3. Direct Objects and Indirect Objects
4. Prepositions, Objects of Prepositions, Prepositional Phrases

Let's break down this sentence into its elements:

Big Jake threw Stinky Petey into the stream.

The verb is *threw* because it shows action. When you ask the verb "Who threw?" or "What threw?" you find the subject. Who threw? Big Jake threw. The subject is *Big Jake*. Big Jake threw whom? He threw Stinky Petey. *Stinky Petey* receives the action of the subject and the verb and is therefore the direct object. The preposition is *into*. Into shows the relationship between threw, Stinky Petey, and stream. We could have used other prepositions. Big Jake could have thrown Stinky Petey over, across, or out of the stream. But the preposition we want here is *into*. The prepositional phrase is *into the stream*. A prepositional phrase begins with a preposition and ends with a noun or pronoun. The noun or pronoun is the object of the preposition. Here the object of the preposition is stream. Later we will discuss all these elements in depth, as well as verbals and clauses serving in place of nouns, pronouns, and objects.

Let us try another sentence:

Big Jake threw Stinky Petey a bar of soap.

The verb is still *threw*. The subject is still *Big Jake*. The direct object is now *bar*. Big Jake threw what? He threw a bar. *Bar* receives the action of the subject and the verb. *Stinky Petey* is now the indirect object. Big Jake threw the bar to whom? To Stinky

Petey. *Stinky Petey* receives the action of Big Jake throwing the bar of soap. *Of soap* is a prepositional phrase.

Eureka! That's all there is to the basic sentence: subject, verb, object, prepositional phrase. Congratulations, crittur. I hereby confer upon you the title of:

✳ **MASTER OF THE SENTENCE** ✳

# Dogs and Ponies Pulling the Travois:

## Identifying Sentence Elements

*"Words ain't much use when a thievin' stranger is galloping away on your horse."*

—Silas Potter—

When Big Jake McLaughlin was a lad new to the mountains, it was Silas Potter who gave him some "words of learning" that stood him in good stead through the years.

"You may growl like a bear and have all the tooth and claw to back you up," Silas Potter said, "but don't figure a fool to back off. If you're goin' t' posture for a fight, you'd better be ready and willing to have at it."

The mountains offered a man absolute freedom from laws, taxes, preachers, and the unnatural notion that a man needs to be reined away from the sins of women and whiskey. For a man who didn't mind sleeping on the earth, there was whiskey and tobacco available and enough wilderness, wild game, willing squaws, and heady mountain winds to feed his appetites.

Many mountain men stayed in the Rockies or on the high prairies through all the seasons of the year. And because summertime pelts were worthless, mostly, the mountain men did little trapping when the days were hot and long. Summer was a time to wander and explore, to make new alliances with the Indians, or cement old friendships. After 1825, summertime meant rendezvous—that festive, rollicking, no-holds-barred gathering of the devil's own.

The very first rendezvous was in early July of 1825 on Randavouze Creek, later known as Henry's Fork of the Green River in southern Wyoming, just north of the Uinta Mountains. The Henry's Fork rendezvous came about because General William Ashley saw a backdoor way to profit from the fur trade. Summertime offered wide, dry prairies across which an enterprising man could roll a packtrain of supplies to the trappers who stayed year-round in the mountains. Ashley was one of the first to realize that the supply-and-buy side of the fur business could be as profitable as trapping itself. Ashley's wagons rolled in loaded with rifles, rifle ball, powder, traps, knives, coffee, sugar, tobacco, whiskey, and mirrors, combs, and trinkets for white man and Indian alike. The wagons rolled out on the return trip loaded with furs that would bring a handsome profit in St. Louis.

That first rendezvous lasted only one day, but it proved a profitable day, indeed, for Ashley. The general paid the trappers an average of three dollars a pound for their furs and carted out almost four and a half tons of beaver pelts worth nearly fifty thousand dollars in St. Louis.

The 1825 rendezvous was a church luncheon compared to subsequent rendezvous. In some ways it was the end of innocence for the mountain man. Future rendezvous were pure diversion, drinking, gambling, storytelling, news-gathering and rumor-spreading, and trading and selling—knives, rifles, horses, and wives—dancing, singing, womanizing, and debauchery in general. No self-respecting mountain man would miss a rendezvous.

---

## SUBJECT ELEMENTS

The subject of a sentence is who or what the sentence is about—usually a noun or pronoun. The verb in the sentence is your key to finding the subject. First identify the verb and then ask the verb who? or what? The verb will answer you, I promise. The answer is the subject. The only thing you have to remember to do is to say the words "who?" or "what?" before you say the verb. Sometimes it's confusing when there's more than one verb in the sentence, but stick with this, crittur. It works.

Stinky Petey is a mountain man.

The verb is *is*. Go ahead, ask who? or what? "What is," or "Who is?" The verb will answer: "Stinky Petey is." *Stinky Petey* is the subject of the sentence. The verb leads you to the subject.

> The squaw tossed Stinky Petey out of her tepee.

The verb is *tossed*. Who tossed? The squaw tossed. By asking "who?" or "what?" before you say the verb, you find the subject of the sentence.

Here, there, where, and everywhere are never subjects of a sentence. Adverbs, conjunctions, transition words, and interjections are never subjects. The subject of a sentence is never found within a prepositional phrase.

The verb often comes before the subject in sentences that begin with here, there, where, or everywhere.

> Everywhere ran antelope stampeding down the draw.

In an interrogative sentence, the subject is often in the middle of the verb.

> Where are you going? (The verb is *are going*. The subject is *you*.)
> Why did Wiley Willie finish his work so fast? (The verb is *did finish*. The subject is *Wiley Willie*.)

Like nouns and pronouns, gerunds, infinitives, phrases, and subordinate clauses can also be subjects of a sentence. (See Verbals and Phrases and Clauses.) In the following sentences, the subject is underlined; the verb is italicized.

> <u>What a mountain man carries in his possible sack</u> *is* about all he'll ever need in the mountains.
> <u>Placing a well-concealed trap on a log that spans a stream</u> *is* highly effective for raccoons and foxes.
> <u>Running away from an angry bear</u> *can be* healthy exercise.

When interrupting words or phrases come between the subject and verb, the subject is never found within the interrupting words. In the following sentences, *chief* and *horses* are the subjects.

> The chief *with the many horses* was Red Cloud. (The chief was Red Cloud.)
> The horses *in the valley* are his. (The horses are his.)

---

To Big Jake rendezvous meant smells—the varied scents and fragrances that filled his spirit to brimming. There were good smells and bad smells and the heady smells that accompanied memories he would carry to his grave.

There was the ammonia-pungent, nostril-wrenching smell of the open latrine trenches that made a man catch and hold his breath. Of course, most mountain men would not actually bother to use a latrine. After the whiskey began to flow freely, one man's campsite was another man's dungpile.

There were the smells of wood smoke, horses, mules, dogs, tobacco, whiskey and whiskey wagons, the rancid, stinking Indians, and the putrid hold-your-breath mountain men. There were other scents, sentient and sensual. The squaws at rendezvous, the young ones—the Crow women, especially—knew how to scent their bodies with natural musk and native fragrances that could drive a man to distraction. Notions of morality, virginity, fidelity, and abstinence were foreign to most Indian women. They seemed shy at first, but there was that bold daring in their dark eyes. Regarded primarily as a working animal and valued as mere chattel by the men of her own clan, many a squaw was happy to take up with a white trapper. Big Jake was happy, too. With the hint of a grin and a sparkle in his eyes, he returned the glances of the shy, uninhibited squaws with their musky, sweet grass scents and their bear-greased hair.

The morning smells at rendezvous were best. In the clean, cold air at dawn's first light was the smell of wood smoke and the wonderful all-the-world-is-right aroma of coffee brewing on the morning fire, the sharp earthy scents of new beginnings, and the smell of buffalo meat or pork bellies sizzling, spitting, and dripping over the dancing flames. On a dank morning, the lowering rain clouds came blowing in on charcoal gray winds from across the prairie. And of a chilly dawn, Big Jake would stand and watch the stiff, gentle sway of the cottonwood and the dark mountain peaks beyond. In his ears would be the wind and the lonesome whisper of the sage, in his nostrils the scent of sweet grass, in his mind the wild imaginings of a mountain man.

---

## *Compound Subject*

When a sentence has two or more subjects, the sentence is said to have a compound subject.

> *Big Jake* and *Jim Bridger* are mountain men.

The verb is *are*. Ask the verb "who?" or "what?" are, and you will find that *Big Jake* and *Jim Bridger* are elements of the compound subject.

## PREDICATE ELEMENTS

The predicate tells about the subject and supports the subject in logic, purpose, and definition. The predicate can be simple or complex, according to what the subject is doing, feeling, or experiencing. Whatever else it does, the predicate must make sense of the sentence.

The predicate itself may contain distinct elements that need understanding:

1. Direct objects and indirect objects
2. Prepositions, objects of prepositions, prepositional phrases

### *Compound Predicate*

When a sentence has two or more verbs expressing the action or state of being of the subject, the sentence is said to have a compound predicate. In the sentences below, the verbs are *loved* and *hated, was* and *grew*. Go ahead, ask the verbs anything you want—just be polite. Who loved? Who hated? Who was? Who grew? The verbs point to *Big Jake* and *Parker Daniels* as the subjects.

> Big Jake loved leisure and hated work.
> Parker Daniels was bitter and grew angry.

### *"Objects" as Part of the Predicate*

For a more comprehensive understanding of objects, the gentle crittur is referred to Verbs and the Objects They Take (page 85). Until we cross that divide, think of objects this way: The subject of a sentence does the action; the object of a sentence receives the action. The verb is in the middle between the subject and the object (most times).

> The Indian hurled the lance.

The verb *hurled* is key to understanding the sentence. Who hurled? The Indian hurled. *Indian* is the subject. Hurled. Hurled what? Hurled the lance. *Lance* is the object receiving the action of the subject and the verb.

Objects are always nouns, pronouns, or strange things pretending to be nouns. Some sentences have both 1) a direct object that receives the action of the subject and verb, and 2) an indirect object that receives the action of the verb and direct object. Other sentences have prepositional phrases with objects of the preposition which belong to, or complement the preposition. Don't be intimidated, gentle crittur; this isn't as difficult as it sounds.

## The Direct Object

To find the direct object of an action verb, again you must first identify the verb. You ask the verb whom? or what? and the verb answers with the direct object. It really is that simple. You just have to remember the order of things. Say the verb first this time, before you say the words *whom* or *what*.

The old scout told another tall tale.

The verb is not only the path to the subject; it is also the path to the object. If you are looking to find the subject, you say the verb last. You ask the verb: "who told?" or "what told?" Your answer is: the *scout* told. *Scout* is the subject. But to find the object, you say the verb first and ask: "told whom?" or "told what?" Your answer is: *tall tale*. *Tall tale* is the direct object.

## The Indirect Object

Now let us look for an indirect object. An indirect object indirectly receives the action from the subject and verb. But first the action must go past the direct object. You cannot have an indirect object unless you first have a direct object.

The old scout told the colonel another tall tale.

We know the verb is *told* and the direct object is *tall tale*. Now, to find the indirect object, you say the verb and direct object together (say the verb first) and ask them: "to whom?" "to what?" "for whom? or "for what?" Told the tall tale to whom? Answer: the *colonel. Colonel* is the indirect object. See how simple this is once you get the order of things?

*Object of the Preposition*
Now—about that pesky object of the preposition. The object of the preposition is simply the noun or pronoun that follows the preposition. The preposition relates that noun or pronoun to other words in the sentence.

(See Prepositions. Better see it now, crittur.)

The old scout told the colonel about half-naked Indians.

*About* is the preposition. *About half-naked Indians* is the prepositional phrase. *Indians* is the object of the preposition—the noun that follows the preposition about. In between the preposition and the noun is *half-naked*, which is an adjective and not a major consideration here. It is the preposition *about* that relates Indians to the other elements in the sentence.

*Compound Objects*

A sentence can contain two or more direct objects, indirect objects, or objects of a preposition. They're called compound objects, but by now you probably figured that out yourself. There's hope for you, crittur.

> Silas Potter hunted *elk* and *buffalo*. (Compound direct object)
> He taught *Big Jake* and *Stinky Petey* survival skills. (Compound indirect object)
> Survival for *mountain man* and *Indian* was a daily endeavor. (Compound object of the preposition)

## Prepositions and Prepositional Phrases

**"Words ain't much use when a thievin' stranger is galloping away on your horse."**

━SILAS POTTER

Back in the 1950s, Del Reeves sang an engaging little country song asking an intriguing question: "Who is the girl wearing nothin' but a smile and a towel in the picture on the billboard in the field near the big old highway?" There are enough prepositions in that song to make a country boy's head spin, not to mention set his heart flutterin'.

So, what is a preposition exactly? A preposition is a word that relates a noun or pronoun to other words in a sentence. That's the definition the grammar books give you. Most grammarians will tell you that

here we are specifically talking about the relationship of the object of the preposition (the noun or pronoun) to other words in the sentence. Mostly, that's
true. But more accurately, a preposition shows the
relationship of verbs to object nouns and object pronouns, and to subject nouns and subject pronouns in
the sentence. In the example below, the preposition
*into* relates Silas Potter's skulking to the Indian
encampment. The preposition *for* links *his looking* to
*his stolen horses.*

> That night Silas Potter skulked into the
> Indian encampment. He was looking for
> his stolen horses.

Many prepositions tell where something is located: on, between, by, under, over, down, across, in,
through, on top of, etc. Some prepositions tell a condition or show a relationship: except, with, without,
like, etc. Other prepositions show references,
absences, or separations: on account of, because, by,
in spite of, etc. Still other prepositions show a time
element: after, before, until, etc. Prepositions do all
these things in relationship to other words in the sentence. The other words can be either nouns, pronouns, or verbs.

If a preposition is not followed by an object noun
or object pronoun, it's probably not a preposition. It's
more likely an errant adverb.

## Common (and Some Uncommon) Prepositions:

aboard
about
above
according to
across
after
against
along
among
around
as
aside from
at
because of
before
behind
below
beneath
beside
between
beyond
but
  (When it means
  "except"—
  otherwise *but* is
  a conjunction.)

by
by means of
by way of
concerning
considering
despite
down
during
except
except for
excepting
for
from
in
in front of
in spite of
instead of
inside
into
like
near
of
off
on

on account of
on top of
onto
out
out of
outside
over
past
prior
since
subsequent to
through
throughout
to
toward
under
underneath
until
up
upon
with
within
without

Prepositions position nouns and pronouns so they make sense in relation to other words. The word *preposition* does what its name says: It pre-positions itself before its object. An object (noun or pronoun) must always follow a preposition, otherwise the preposition is alone and naked—a faux pas, to be sure.

Stinky Petey, where you at?

This is wrong because the preposition *at* cannot stand alone at the end of the sentence. It must be followed by an object noun or pronoun. Let's try it again.

Where you at, stupid?

Close, but still not correct. Used here, *stupid* is not an object. It is not even an adjective. It is an appellation. The preposition still needs an object noun or pronoun. Let's try some examples to show the difference. The first sentence in each pair of sentences below ends in a preposition. The second sentence in each pair has been recast to correct the error.

She's the person I spoke to.
She's the person to whom I spoke.

That's the horse I sat on.
That's the horse on which I sat.

St. Louis was the town I was born in.
St Louis was the town in which I was born.

As a matter of practicality, a crittur will find it almost impossible to strictly adhere to the rule about prepositions not ending a sentence. The best of coons have tried and failed on this score. At least try to never have a naked preposition end a sentence. That's what an object is for.

*Prepositional Phrases*

A prepositional phrase begins with a preposition and ends with the object of the preposition—usually a noun or pronoun. Words, if any, that describe the object of the preposition come between the preposition and the object. The words in between the preposition and its object are part of the prepositional phrase.

The trapper chased the cougar *off its kill.*

The prepositional phrase is *off its kill.* The phrase begins with the preposition *off* and ends with the object noun *kill.* The preposition *off* has more to do with the verb *chased* than with the nouns *trapper* or *kill.* Still, it shows a relationship between the two nouns.

Sometimes two prepositional phrases follow one after the other. In the following example there are two prepositional phrases.

The other gamblers chased Parker Daniels
*along the length of the river.*

*Along the length* is an adverb prepositional phrase modifying the verb *chased*. *Of the river* is an adjective prepositional phrase describing the noun *length*.

> **"Parker Daniels never understood about honor. Honor's only honor when it's used. Honor ain't somethin' a man keeps in reserve. Yesterday's honor ain't nuthin' when the sun comes up on a new day. And this morning's honor, when it's past, won't get you through the comin' night."**
>
> ⌐Silas Potter

*Subjects, Predicates, and Prepositional Phrases*
As stated earlier, the subject of a sentence is never found inside a prepositional phrase. In the following sentences, the prepositional phrases are italicized, and little remains of each sentence but the subject and verb:

*Down the valley* ran he.

After you disregard the prepositional phrase, all you have left is: *he* as the subject, *ran* as the verb.

Big Jake, *along with the soldiers*, charges *up the hill.*

After you disregard the prepositional phrases, all you have left is *Big Jake* as the subject and *charges* as the verb.

Big Jake and the soldiers charge up the hill.

If you can recognize prepositional phrases, and you know your parts of speech, that only leaves *Big Jake* and *soldiers* as the compound subject and the verb *charge* as the predicate. Ain't this simple, crittur?

## APPOSITIVES

It was Silas Potter who years before had taken a young Jake McLaughlin "under his toot-lage" and taught him the way the stick floats.

"If you want the big fur company to stake you and map out for you the best areas to set your traps, go sign on with them. Take what they give you and do their bidding and go fetch their pelts. But if your heart is free and fearless, if you trust your wits and your courage, go strike out on your own and wander the mountains alone. As a Free Trapper you will suffer some, sure, but you will walk against the sky. You will camp by your own fire. You will breathe the cool mountain breezes. You will live until you die."

An appositive is a word, or group of words, that describes, clarifies, modifies, identifies, or in some way gives more meaning to a noun.

> *A trustworthy guide,* Jim Bridger knew the mountains well.

*Guide* is in apposition with *Jim Bridger*.

An appositive works best when it immediately follows the noun it modifies. Nonrestrictive appositives are those which can be omitted from the sentence without changing the meaning of the sentence. Use commas to set off nonrestrictive appositives that add extraneous information about the noun.

> Big Jake's sworn enemy, *Sagebrush Sam*, came into camp that night.
>
> To alert his warriors, Yellow Knife, *the shaman*, whistled the low melodic call of a whippoorwill.

Restrictive appositives are an integral part of the sentence and should not be set off with commas. The following sentences would not make sense without the restrictive appositives, therefore commas are not needed.

> The mountain man *Jim Bridger* was a legendary figure well before his twenty-fifth birthday.
>
> Though not held in the same regard, Bridger's friend *Big Jake* was equally talked about over many a campfire.
>
> Are you talking about Joe *the trapper* or Joe *the guide*?

By the omission of commas in the first sentence, the writer is implying that there could be no other mountain man who was a legendary figure so early in life. Jim Bridger is the only name that could fit here, so it is a necessary part of the sentence and should not be set off by commas. Of course, the writer is mistaken about young Jim Bridger, but you get the idea. That logic holds true for all three sentences.

Deft use of appositives tightens your writing and moves the reader along. The second sentence below is a good example of an effective appositive.

> Silas Potter was Big Jake's mentor and friend. He taught Big Jake the Indian languages and the Indian ways.
>
> Big Jake's mentor and friend, Silas Potter, taught him the Indian languages and the Indian ways.

## Types of Sentences

Locoweed Louie had a problem with words because he had a problem with logic. It was said, when the good Lord was passing out smarts, Locoweed Louie thought He said "darts."

"Don't want nuthin' too sharp," says Locoweed Louie.

And the next day when the Lord began to pass out luck, Locoweed Louie thought he said "duck." That's another story.

Locoweed Louie was a likeable enough cuss, but no one could ever accuse him of possessing the necessary number of brain cells that could carry over beyond one place column. But he must have known something, for he was often seen smiling to himself for no apparent reason. Having no apparent reason was why Locoweed Louie did a lot of things.

Yet, somehow Locoweed Louie was good with whiskey, and not a coon ever thought it was liquor ever turned him fool of the day. No one had the answer to that one.

With oxen pulling the big wagons, the traders carted in the whiskey in sixty-three gallon hogsheads. There was good whiskey for the forts and settlements, and watered down whiskey laced with tobacco, molasses, and capsicum for trade with the Indians and mountain men. Locoweed Louie had little in the way of brains, but even he avoided the bad whiskey. Maybe he just never acquired a taste for it.

"I hates Injun whiskey," Locoweed Louie would say. "I wouldn't buy it if you gave it to me."

---

## Compound Sentences

A compound sentence consists of two independent clauses—two complete sentences—joined by a comma and conjunction, or by a semicolon. (See Conjunctions.) (See Semicolons.) Compound sentences are not inherently superior to simple sentences, they just make you sound intelligent if you couple them properly. But you can sound pretty dumb if you stretch the reader's imagination too thin. The sentences following are probably at the edge—tolerable if a crittur can get past them without stumbling over the words or meaning.

> The sun melted into deep purple pools beyond the western mountains, and the night spread its inky shadows through the forest.
>
> The night wind howled through the trees; we lit our campfire.

## Inverted Sentences

The subject of a sentence (usually a noun or pronoun) generally comes before the verb in the sentence.

> Big Jake married an unfortunate looking woman who never let him out of her sight.

*Big Jake* is the subject; *married* is the verb. This is your standard sentence structure with the subject before the verb. If you kept to this structure throughout your writing, you would be hacking out some pretty boring stuff. To liven up your writing, you may want to put your verb before your subject. When the verb comes before the subject, the sentence is said to be inverted. Stylistically, an inverted sentence can strike a dramatic tone.

> Above the valley hung the clouds of war.
>
> Is life so dear or peace so sweet?
>
> What a productive trapper was he!

In the last sentence, the subject *he* comes after the "be" verb *was*. Remember to use the subject pronoun, not the object pronoun after a "be" verb. (See Subject Pronouns.)

The verb often comes before the subject in sentences that begin with here, there, where, or everywhere. Remember here, there, where, or everywhere are never the subjects of sentences. To find the subject of an inverted sentence, you do the same thing you do with any other sentence. You agonize over the verb. First identify the verb and ask "who?" or "what?" Remember to re-invert or recast the sentence in your head.

Here is the sidewinder who stole my horse.

The verb is *is*. Who is? Sidewinder is. Sidewinder is here who stole my horse. Or, in traditional sentence construction: The sidewinder who stole my horse is here.

There are those redskins who cheated me out of my plunder.

The verb is *are*. Who are? Redskins are. Redskins are there who cheated me out of my plunder. The redskins who cheated me out of my plunder are there.

See, crittur, how easy this is when it's broken down into simple horse sense?

### *The Clipped Sentence*

A clipped sentence is not really a sentence because it lacks a subject, predicate, or both. Clipped sentences should be avoided, but sometimes their effect is irresistible.

No way!

*No way!* has no subject and no verb, but the reader gets the message unmistakably.

A clipped sentence is acceptable if the emphasis is justified and if you do not overdo it. A serious writer probably writes a clipped sentence maybe once every twenty years.

She counted on Big Jake to be there on their wedding day. Not so.

That was easy. That's about all the sentence elements you'll ever need to identify. Congratulations, crittur. I hereby confer upon you the title of:

### ❄ KEEPER OF THE DOGS AND PONIES ❄

# THE WAY THE STICK FLOATS:

## Subject-Verb Agreement

Sagebrush Sam had a nasty shrew of a squaw, given to meanness and obstinance, and as implacable as a rattlesnake in full strike. She had a short temper and a foul mouth. When angry—and she was always angry—she was wont to brandish, swing, or throw pots and pans at anyone who crossed her path; hence, her name, Iron Skillet. The only endearing quality Iron Skillet possessed was laziness; she would sleep most of the day.

One night, either through design gone wrong, foolhardy bravado, unimaginable stupidity, sheer orneriness, or more likely heavy drinking, Big Jake stole Iron Skillet away from Sagebrush Sam. Stealing her wasn't so much a coup for Big Jake, it was more a coup that she even went with him, for no one could make Iron Skillet do anything she did not want to do.

Big Jake may not have been entirely happy with his new woman, but he was loath to complain, especially in her presence. In his own perverse way, Big Jake was proud to boast of having the stupidest dog, the dullest knife, the slowest horse, and the meanest, ugliest woman west of St. Louis.

If Sagebrush Sam brooded over his loss, you couldn't tell it behind his smile.

---

The old trappers would use line or a small chain to secure a "float stick" to a beaver trap. If a beaver swam away with the heavy trap clamped to its leg, the float stick would show where in the deep water the drowned beaver ended up. In mountain man jargon, knowing the way the stick floats grew to mean knowledge of the wilderness skills necessary for survival in the mountains. A man who knew the way the stick floats knew what he needed to know; he was savvy; he knew what was "happening," what was going on. The term was used to describe only the most experienced, resourceful, and skillful mountain men.

When it comes to American grammar, a crittur needs to know the way the stick floats.

Making the subject and verb in the same sentence agree is simple enough. All you have to do is identify the subject of your sentence, ascertain whether the subject is singular or plural, understand the person in which the subject is written, and not be confused by intervening words, phrases, and dependent clauses between the subject and the verb. Whoa, crittur! Let's start at the beginning.

Subject-verb agreement simply means that the subject and verb in your sentence are both singular or both plural and both in the same person. Tread carefully here, crittur; this gets tricky. Let's take person first.

## PERSONS

Persons are personal pronoun forms that directly relate to nouns. (Nouns are not designated in terms of person.) A verb must agree in person with the subject of a sentence. For example, you cannot use the first person pronoun *I* with the second person verb *are*. The following is obviously incorrect.

I *are* a mountain man.

|            | Singular    | Plural      |
|------------|-------------|-------------|
| 1st Person | I, me       | we, us      |
| 2nd Person | you         | you         |
| 3rd Person | he, she, it | they, them  |

### *First Person*

When one is speaking or writing in the first person, he or she is referring to himself or herself by using the following pronouns: *I, me* (singular) or *we, us* (plural). Subjects in the first person need first person verbs.

I *am* a mountain man.
We *are* trappers.

## Second Person

The person whom a writer or speaker is addressing is the second person. There are two second person pronouns, and they are both *you*: *you* singular and *you* plural. Subjects in the second person need second person verbs.

> You *are* a horse thief.
> You *are* scoundrels.

## Third Person

The person or thing spoken about by an impersonal, omniscient, or unidentified writer is the third person. The third person pronouns are: *he, she, it, him, her* (singular), or *they, them* (plural). Subjects in the third person need third person verbs.

> She *is* a beautiful Indian maiden.
> They all *want* to marry her.

Present tense verbs are the same for first, second, and third person—except third person singular.

**First Person:** I shoot. We shoot.
**Second Person:** You shoot.
**Third Person (singular):** He, she, or it shoots. Wit-less Winslow, Wiley Willie, or Locoweed Louie shoots. The scout shoots.
**Third person (plural):** They shoot.

# NUMBER

When we speak of the *number* of a noun, pronoun, verb, etc., we are speaking of singular or plural. Most nouns are made plural by adding an *s*. Present tense verbs are made plural by omitting the *s*. A verb must agree in *number* with the subject of a sentence. If the subject is singular, the verb must be singular. If the subject is plural, the verb must be plural.

> The Indian (singular noun) rides (singular verb) away.
>
> Two Indians (plural noun) ride (plural verb) away.

Some verbs have different forms for singular and plural.

> He (singular pronoun) does (singular verb) his job.
>
> They (plural pronoun) do (plural verb) their jobs.
>
> She (singular pronoun) has (singular verb) integrity.
>
> We (plural pronoun) have (plural verb) integrity.

A plural subject, or a compound subject joined by *and*, needs a plural verb.

> The scout (singular subject) goes (singular verb) wandering.

The scouts (plural subject) go (plural verb) wandering.

Stinky Petey (singular subject) is (singular verb) in need of a bath.

Stinky Petey and Big Jake (compound subject) are (plural verb) foul smelling critturs.

Within close environs, they (plural subject) are (plural verb) known to make your eyes water.

Agreement in number between the subject and verb is not an issue in the past and future verb tenses. The verb remains the same regardless of whether the subject is singular or plural. But present tense verbs, however, have two verb forms.

| | Past | Future |
|---|---|---|
| **Singular** | Big Jake *bought* tobacco. | Big Jake *will buy* whiskey. |
| **Plural** | The men *bought* tobacco. | The men *will buy* whiskey. |

| | Present |
|---|---|
| **Singular** | Big Jake *buys* tobacco. |
| **Plural** | The men *buy* tobacco. |

## Each *Is Tricky*

*Anyone, anybody, everyone, everybody, no one, nobody, someone, somebody, each, either,* and *neither* are singular pronouns and take singular verbs. However, the word *each* after a plural subject does not make the verb singular. The verb stays plural.

The <u>trackers</u> each *have* their own method.
(Trappers, too.)

When you use the word *each* before a singular noun, or before a prepositional phrase with a plural object, use a singular verb. Now a smart crittur like you isn't always satisfied with a rule like that. You want to know why. It's that way because the word *each* before a singular noun is an adjective. *Each* before a prepositional phrase with a plural object is a pronoun. Adjectives are never subjects of a sentence; pronouns can be subjects of a sentence.

Each <u>tracker</u> (singular subject) *has* (singular verb) his own method.
<u>Each</u> (singular subject) of the trackers *has* (singular verb) his own method.

## Each *and* Every *in a Compound Subject*

When a compound subject begins with *each* or *every*, the verb must be singular. When *each* follows a compound subject joined by *and*, the verb must be plural.

Every trapper, hunter, and scout *was* present at Rendezvous.
Each Indian and white man *was* welcomed.
Indian and white man each *were* welcomed.

## All, Any, None, What *and Subject-Verb Agreement*

The pronouns *all*, *any*, *none*, and *what* can be singular or plural depending on the context of the sentence.

If you say *all, any, none,* or *what* of something and you denote a collective oneness, you need a singular verb. If you say *all, any, none,* or *what* of these things—and you denote many things, you need a plural verb.

The word *all* can be a pronoun, adjective, noun, adverb, maybe even a conjunction if I work at it hard enough. The pronoun *all* presents special problems with subject-verb agreement. As with most things grammatical, it all comes down to the writer's mental clarity. When you write *all,* what does all stand for—what word or words does *all* replace?

*All* is singular and requires a singular verb when *all* indicates a conceptual oneness—a total, no matter how many individual things are included.

> All that glisters is not gold.

Every single thing that glisters is not gold. Actually, that's how Shakespeare wrote it. Later, lesser men and city dudes changed it to "all that glitters" or "all that glistens."

In its singular sense, *all* means "the total" (the whole), "everything" (the total as one entity), or "the only thing."

> All I had is lost.
> In summertime all I do is trap each day and
> fight off mosquitoes, snakes, bears, and
> Indians.

In the first sentence above, *all* I had—the total—

is lost—and we need a singular verb. In the second sentence, *all* means "the only thing" and requires the singular verb *is*.

> Ten dollars is all I lost.

In the sentence above, we need a singular verb because we conceptualize ten dollars as one sum total of a small amount. We could say, "Five hundred dollars is all I lost." Again, we consider the five hundred as one sum total.

---

Trapping was best in late autumn and spring when the pelts were thick and sleek. Winters were unproductive once the streams froze, so mountain men wintered-in somewhere with their squaws, a supply of "bacca," whiskey, or rum, plenty of wood for the fire, and plenty of venison, elk, and buffalo.

It was useless to trap in the summertime; summer pelts were of poor quality. Summers were best for socializing, visiting friendly Indian villages, and of course, gathering at rendezvous to squander away a season's worth of pelts on whiskey and rum, frolicsome dalliances with uninhibited squaws, and merry-making in general and particular.

---

> *All* I get for my troubles is a few summer pelts.

Again, *all* means "the only thing" and requires the singular verb *is*.

*All* is plural and requires a plural verb when *all* refers to separate, distinct individual items.

> All ten of the dollars are gone.
> All the good guys are gone. (All these good
>   guys are gone.)

Here we need a plural verb because we consider the loss in terms of several individual items—ten one dollar bills—and we regard the loss as a comparatively, significantly, costly, consequential matter including more than one component—in fact ten components, ten dollars.

*All* is plural and requires a plural verb when *all* is all-inclusive of individual things that can be counted, or when it means all of several things. Again, it comes down to the clarity in the mind of the writer.

> All the mountain men *were* adventurers.
>   (plural verb)
> All the good days *are* gone. (plural verb)

The same rules apply to the pronoun *any*. *Any* is singular and requires a singular verb when *any* indicates a conceptual oneness—a total, no matter how many individual things are included. In its singular sense, *any* means "the total" (the whole), "everything" (the total as one entity), or "the only thing."

> Castoreum was carried in a horn, distinguished from a powder horn, certainly. Any a trapper acquired was a valuable commodity. (Any amount of castoreum *was...*)
>
> The soldiers are well trained. Any are suitable for the challenges ahead. (Any of them *are* suitable...)

The pronoun *none* can be singular or plural depending on the context of the sentence. In the first sentence below, *none* is singular meaning "no one" or "not one." In the second sentence, *none* is plural meaning "not any."

> None is ready to surrender.
> None are ready to surrender.

The pronoun *what* can be either singular or plural depending upon the noun it is replacing and the context of the sentence.

> What *are* you saying? (plural)
> What *is* this? (singular)

When *what* as a subject of a sentence takes two verbs (a compound predicate), both verbs and the subject must all agree in number. This is another tricky one. You cannot have one verb singular and the other verb plural.

Correct: What makes Jim Bridger a great mountain man is his unfailing instincts. (The verbs *makes* and *is* are both singular.)

Since *what* can take the place of a singular or plural noun, the verb's "number" determines your meaning. If you are writing about Bridger's instincts in a plural sense, the following sentence is also correct—although no self-respecting mountain man would ever write such a sentence.

Correct: What make Jim Bridger a great mountain man are his unfailing instincts. (The verbs *make* and *are* are both plural. To affirm that this sentence is correct, let us recast it: His unfailing instincts are what make Jim Bridger a great mountain man.)

Correct: Big Jake reports what seem to be twenty Indians riding hard toward our camp. (This sentence is correct because the verb *seem* and the noun *Indians* are both plural.)

Incorrect: Big Jake reports what seems to be twenty Indians riding hard toward our camp. (This sentence is incorrect because the verb *seems* is singular and the noun *Indians* is plural. Twenty Indians seem to be riding toward our camp.)

Let's try it one more way:

Correct: Big Jake reports what seems to be an Indian riding hard toward our camp. (This sentence is correct because the verb *seems* and the noun *Indian* are both singular. An Indian seems to be riding toward our camp.)

━━━━━◆•◆◆•◆━━━━━

Rendezvous was always an adventure for Big Jake, though the big man was born a loner. It wasn't that he didn't enjoy the company of other trappers, Indians, traders, company men, and even the amusement of encountering a stray preacher once in a while. As Big Jake would tell it, he was just used to scratching wherever it itched. So, at any rendezvous, Big Jake could be found camped out on the fringes of the encampment. With bands of marauding Indians and the occasional grizzly wandering about, some other trappers would figure the fringes weren't the safest place to spread their blanket out, alone and away from the throng. But the big guy reckoned it was precisely that remoteness that kept things as safe as he wanted them to be. And it was all right out there alone sleeping on the wet earth or in the dry, dusty grass with the ants and beetles crawling, biting, and gnawing, and the boring-into-the-skin little things flying and hopping, or carried along on the breeze.

Big Jake loved the lonesome crackle of the fire. Out there in that quiet solitude, the cold, silvery moonglow was company and comfort to a lonely man. Out away from it all, the wind blew for him alone, and for him alone the clouds brooded and scudded across the night sky. Sitting cross-legged on the earth, his was the familiar pipeful of tobacco with its wreaths of white smoke rising to the stars. And out there, for him alone the mornings broke clean and sweet, scattering the somber darkness over the westward peaks. Each waking morning was a new adventure, whether alone or with a squaw warm beside him, the dank, dark breezes chilling his bones and renewing his spirits. Out on the fringes, away from it all, was as close to heaven as a man like Big Jake could get.

---

## *You* and *I* and the Verbs They Keep Company With

Maybe I'm showing my age here, crittur, but "keeping company" used to mean what you young'uns call "going steady." Well, maybe that's changed, too. Okay, how about "wooing." Everyone knows what wooing is. We used to call it "pitching woo." Just so we're all talking about the same thing here—it's when you take a gal and go out in the moonlight with her and pour out your soul to her and generally make a total ass of yourself—especially if your so-called friends are out there hiding in the nearby bushes listening to every word you say. I'm here to tell you, the following day and for years afterwards you're going to hear all about it in glorious detail. Man, if that ain't a sorry kettle o' buffla guts!

*You* always takes a plural verb (even when *you* is

singular). *I* always takes a plural verb except with *am* and *was*. *Am* and *was* are the only singular verb forms used with *I*. Don't ask me why. It's the law west of the Rockies—and in at least three states and the Kansas Territory.

*Sings* is a singular verb. *Sing* is a plural verb. Yet we use the plural verb when we say: *I sing* or *you* (singular) *sing*.

> I sing…we sing
> You sing
> He sings…one girl sings…Willie sings…
> They sing…two girls sing…Willie and
>     Waylon sing…

*Has* is a singular verb. We say: *he*, *she*, or *it* has.

*Have* is a plural verb. We say: *we* or *they* have. Yet we say: *I have*, not *I has*.

We say *I go*, not *I goes—I learn*, not *I learns*.

Sometimes we say: *I do*. (That one can come back to bite you.)

The second person *you*, either as a singular or plural pronoun, always takes a plural verb.

> You *have*…you *go*…you *learn*…Yes, you do.

Imperative sentences always take a plural verb. That's where the "you and I" part of this begins. That's because the subject of an imperative sentence is usually a person directly addressed or the pronoun *you*. Even when *you* is not actually stated, *you* is understood.

> Go right away and tell the colonel!

This imperative sentence is really saying: "You, go right away and tell the colonel!" When a writer uses the second person personal pronoun *you*, he may be writing about you as one person, you as a group of people, or you in reference to people in general. *You* (whether singular or plural) always takes a plural verb. Even if you address one individual by name, the verb is plural.

> Billy Joe, go (not goes) right away and tell the colonel! (Billy Joe, you go right away…)

Now let us introduce the pronoun *I* into the equation. When using the first person personal pronoun *I*, a writer can have a singular subject with a plural verb. In fact, the pronoun *I* only takes two singular verbs: *am* and *was*. All other verbs accompanying *I* are plural verbs. In the example below, *I* is singular, but the verb *hear* is plural.

> I often hear a lone wolf howl its woes to a star-studded sky.
>
> I go… (singular subject, plural verb)
> I believe… (singular subject, plural verb)
> I hunt… (singular subject, plural verb)
> I trap… (singular subject, plural verb)

## COLLECTIVE NOUNS

Collective nouns designate groups and are usually

treated as singular requiring a singular verb.

**Some Collective Nouns**

class

club

family

couple

total

The class *is* out to recess. (singular verb)

The family *is* here. (singular verb)

The Lions Club *is* meeting in the cafeteria.
(singular verb)

Not all collective nouns take a singular verb, and a writer must be confident of his meaning when pairing collective nouns with verbs. Some collective nouns denote the entire group as one entity, requiring a singular verb. Other collective nouns denote the individuals within the group, requiring a plural verb. The writer must be sure in his own mind exactly to whom or to what he is referring. Here are some guidelines, crittur:

★ Using *the* before a collective noun usually indicates the verb should be singular.

★ Using *a* or *an* before a collective noun usually indicates the verb should be plural.

★ The word *of* after the collective noun may also indicate a plural verb is required.

★ Using both *a* before and *of* after a collective noun is usually a pretty sure signal a plural verb is needed.

The total *is* staggering. (singular verb)

A total of eighty-seven men *are* dead. (plural verb)

The couple *survives* on wild game and berries. (singular verb)

A couple of Indians *survive* on pemmican. (plural verb)

The majority *is* not always right. (singular verb)

A majority of mountain men *were* aware of that fact. (plural verb)

The number *is* huge. (singular verb)

A number of them *are* valiant. (plural verb)

An assemblage *is* here to see Big Jake. (singular verb)

An assemblage of seven big guys with guns and a rope *are* here to see Big Jake. (plural verb)

## Sum Totals as One Entity

The rules here get a tad slippery, but if you keep a clear head, it's not so confusing. It comes down to a coon knowing what he means and meaning what he knows, or says, or something. All right, let's get through this.

When the total sum of something is indicated, use a singular verb.

Three square meals *is* a luxury to a mountain man.

Bacon and eggs *is* a good breakfast on a frosty morning.

Twenty dollars *is* a bargain price.

Five grouse *is* plenty for a hearty soup.

Jacobs & Company *is* a fine outfitter.

When you are indicating individual entities within the total, use a plural verb.

The bacon and eggs *are* fresh.

Twenty one dollar bills *are* on the table.

Five grouse *are* in the soup.

## ADDITIONAL MATTERS TO CONSIDER

### *Verbs before the Subject Noun*

When your verb comes before your subject, first identify your verb and determine its agreement with your subject. (See Inverted Sentences.)

*Profiting* from the illegal sale of whiskey to the Indians was *Big Jake* himself. (The singular subject is *Big Jake*. The singular verb is *was profiting*.)

*Attempting to* cross through hostile Indian territory were two *trappers*. (The plural subject is *trappers*. The plural verb is *were attempting*.)

## *Fractions before a Noun*

When you use a fraction before a noun, use a verb that agrees in number with the noun.

> Two-thirds of the *men are* down with dysentery. (plural verb)
>
> Three-quarters of the *medicine is* gone. (singular verb)

## *Verbs Taking Special Form*

When discussing subject-verb agreement, we must consider how the verbs *be*, *do*, and *have* take special forms when singular and plural. Remember the "be" verb is expressed eight ways: *am, is, are, was, were, be, being, been*.

|      | Singular | Plural |
|------|----------|--------|
| be   | am, is   | are    |
|      | was      | were   |
| do   | does     | do     |
|      | did      | did    |
| have | had      | have   |
|      | had      | had    |

> Jedediah Smith *was* the most traveled of the mountain men.
>
> A beaver trap *does* its job by drowning the beaver.
>
> Mountain men generally *have* short life spans.

However, when any of the *be*, *do*, or *have* verbs are

used as helping (auxiliary) verbs, the *be*, *do*, or *have* verbs determine the number (singular or plural) of the verb to agree with the number (singular of plural) of the subject. The main verb does not change.

> Singular: Stinky Petey *is riding* hard.
> Plural: The Kiowa *are riding* hard after him.

> Singular: Stinky Petey *does ride* fast, indeed.
> Plural: The Indians *do ride* fast, too.

> Singular: Big Jake *has heard* tales of gold in the Black Hills.
> Plural: The Sioux *have heard* tales of the white man's greed.

Some helping verbs (such as *can*, *will*, *may*) never change whether the subject of the sentence is singular or plural.

> Singular: He *will* sleep.
> Plural: They *will* sleep.

> Singular: He *can* (or *may*) go.
> Plural: They *can* (or *may*) go.

## COMPOUND SUBJECTS AND SUBJECT-VERB AGREEMENT

When one coon comes visiting another coon's diggin's, a smart coon keeps a wary eye on the visitor. Is it a friendly visit, or is some thievin' trouble in the works? When two coons come calling, you've got compound nouns and compound danger. Keep a sharp eye, crittur. But it's nothing you can't handle.

A compound subject joined by *and* needs a plural verb. Compound subjects connected by *either...or*, or *neither...nor* need a singular verb.

> The traps and the bait *are* ready.
> The trapper and the guide *are* here.
> Either a bent rifle barrel or bad shooting *is* your problem.
> Neither the trapper nor the guide *is* here.

Compound subjects introduced by *each* and *every* take a singular verb. When *each* follows a plural subject or a compound subject joined by *and*, the verb must be plural.

> Each mountain man and Indian scout *is* here.
> Every man and woman *is* here.
> Mountain man and Indian scout each *are* here.

When a compound subject is joined by *or* or *nor*, take special notice. When both subjects are singular, the verb is singular. When both subjects are plural, the verb is plural.

> A <u>gun</u> or a <u>knife</u> *is* all a mountain man ever needs.
> <u>Guns</u> or <u>knives</u> *are* all a mountain man ever needs.
> Neither a <u>gun</u> nor a <u>knife</u> *was* ever enough

to stop Big Jake when he got his Irish up.
Neither <u>guns</u> nor <u>knives</u> *were* enough to
stop Big Jake when he got his Irish up.
<u>Stinky Petey</u> or <u>Big Jake</u> *is* the cause of that
smell.

When the elements of a compound subject are
mixed in number (one subject singular and the other
subject plural), the subject element closest to the
verb determines whether the verb is singular or plural. When the subject closest to the verb is singular,
use a singular verb. When the subject closest to the
verb is plural, use a plural verb.

Neither the two <u>men</u>, nor the <u>boy</u> *is* here.
Neither the <u>boy</u>, nor the two <u>men</u> *are* here.

Twenty angry <u>wildcats</u> or one angry <u>wife</u>
*was* enough to scare any mountain man.
One angry <u>wife</u> or twenty angry <u>wildcats</u>
*were* enough to scare any mountain
man.
Neither <u>words</u> nor a <u>smile</u> *is* enough to
charm a woman scorned.
Neither a <u>smile</u> nor <u>words</u> *are* enough to
charm a woman scorned.

## *Not...only, But...also, But...to*
Use the same rule when subjects are positioning
themselves around *not...only*, *but...also*, and
*but...too*. Again, the subject closest to the verb determines whether the verb is singular or plural.

Not only the <u>horses</u> but also the <u>wagon</u> *was* gone. (…but the wagon also was gone.)
Not only the <u>wagon</u>, but also the <u>horses</u> *were* gone. (…but the horses, too, were gone.)

## *Phrases or Clauses between the Subject and the Verb*

Phrases or clauses that come between the subject and the verb should not affect subject-verb agreement.

**Some examples of words that come between the subject and its verb:**

along with
as well as
believed to be
functioning as
in addition to
including
in conjunction with
together with
up to and including

<u>Soft-Headed Sylvester</u>, along with several hunters, *was* the first to enter camp that night. (Singular <u>subject</u>, singular *verb*)

Do not be confused when the subject is followed by a phrase whose object is different in number from the subject. The verb agrees with the subject, not the object.

The <u>feathers</u> of the eagle *were* seen through the foliage. (plural <u>subject</u>, plural *verb*)

One <u>set</u> of tracks *was* more distinct than the others. (singular <u>subject</u>, singular *verb*)

A mountain man's <u>possessions</u>, all bundled inside his possible sack, *were* all he carried. (plural <u>subject</u>, plural *verb*)

The <u>status</u> of those reports and inventories *is* unknown. (singular <u>subject</u>, singular *verb*)

The <u>value</u> of his pelts *was* high. (singular <u>subject</u>, singular *verb*)

The beaver <u>pelts</u>, sleek and glossy, *are* commanding eight to ten dollars each. (plural <u>subject</u>, plural *verb*)

<u>Each</u> of the beaver pelts, sleek and glossy, *is* commanding eight to ten dollars. (singular <u>subject</u>, singular *verb*)

<u>One</u> in three mountain men *is* fifty percent crazy. (singular <u>subject</u>, singular *verb*)

The <u>reasons</u> for the Indian raid *were*... (plural <u>subject</u>, plural *verb*)

The <u>reason</u> Indians paint their faces *is*... (singular <u>subject</u>, singular *verb*)

<u>One</u> of the scouts *is*... (singular <u>subject</u>, singular *verb*)

The season's <u>haul</u> of furs *is* huge. (singular <u>subject</u>, singular *verb*)

Twenty <u>firearms</u>, including one Hawken rifle, *are*... (plural <u>subject</u>, plural *verb*)

## *Watch out for Contractions*

Watch out for contractions.

> Incorrect: Here's the bullets. (*Here's* is a contraction of *here is*. "Here is the bullets" is wrong because the plural subject <u>bullets</u> needs a plural verb—*are*. Remember *here, where, there, everywhere* are never subjects.)
>
> Correct: Here are the bullets.

Wagh! You've learned subject-verb agreement. Good going, crittur. I hereby confer upon you the title of:

### ⁕ Lord of the Float Stick ⁕

# Civilizing Nouns, Verbs, and Other Wild Things

---

*"Honor is the only thing of value a man really has."*

⌐ SILAS POTTER ⌐

---

"The fur company takes care of the fur company, and the trapper takes care of the trapper," Silas Potter told Big Jake. "That's the nature of things. Still, it's best to be known by your word. Honor is the only thing of value a man really has."

Big Jake was the problem in his relationship with Iron Skillet. The problem was, he didn't want to be in the relationship. Still, Iron Skillet had her sweet moments, most often when she was wild on whiskey. Those times Big Jake would hide from her affections. But invariably, Iron Skillet would find him, and the next morning he'd be roughed up pretty good.

"Ah, civilized humanity," he'd say philosophically to himself. Of course, Iron Skillet could never be the former, and she had little claim to the latter.

---

Similarly, there are relationships in grammar and usage that defy logic. You just must learn the rules, crittur. In grammar, as with women, rules are not always easy to understand. As with Iron Skillet, it's best not to get caught breaking the rules.

All right, back to basics.

## Nouns

A noun is a word that names a person, place, thing, or idea. Nouns serve as subjects of a sentence, direct and indirect objects, predicate nouns, or objects of a preposition. But nouns are nothing, really. They lay low, den-up, laze around, just dormant until they want to be seen or heard, or until they want to come out and play. Then they come around looking for verbs. Verbs are where the action is.

There are proper nouns as distinguished from common nouns. A common noun names any ordinary, garden-variety person, place, thing, or idea. A proper noun identifies a person, place, thing, or idea with a particular name attached. Common nouns are like wild mustangs or newborn babies. They are what they are, and that's all that they are until you give them a name. You following this, crittur?

Proper nouns are capitalized.

| **Common Nouns** | **Proper Nouns** |
| --- | --- |
| city | St. Louis |
| man | Sam Jones |
| pistol | Colt |
| state | Virginia |
| boy | Tommy |
| automobile | Ford |

When you write proper nouns consisting of several words, capitalize only the important words. Do not capitalize prepositions.

> Port-au-Prince
> District of Columbia

## *Proper Nouns as Adjectives*

Some nouns (plural, singular, or possessive) serve as adjectives:

> dog days
> states' rights

When proper nouns serve as adjectives, they need to remain capitalized:

> Chinese food
> Italian accent
> American ingenuity

(See Proper Adjectives.)

## *Concrete Nouns and Abstract Nouns*

Concrete nouns are things you can see, touch, chew on, or bang on. Abstract nouns are things you cannot see, touch, chew on, or bang on. Generally, concrete nouns can get a man hurt; abstract nouns can get a man hanged. That's because ideas are dangerous. But you'll learn that, crittur, as you get older and ideas come into your head at random times for better or worse.

| Concrete Nouns | Abstract Nouns |
| --- | --- |
| war drum | courage |
| rifle | patriotism |
| buffalo jerky | honor |
| woman | femininity |

Abstract nouns are ideas and concepts. Thinking of ideas and concepts and feeling emotions are actions represented by verbs.

The thought is the noun: probity, loyalty, honor, courage.

Thinking the thought is the verb: consider, determine, wonder, dream.

> My *decision* is to get out before the Indians get here. (noun)
> You *decide* whether or not you are going with us. (verb)

The emotion is the noun: worry, dread, sorrow.

Feeling the emotion is the verb: worrying, dreading, grieving.

> I *worry* about you. (verb)
> *Worry* never helps. (noun)

## *Possessive Nouns*

Iron Skillet was the Blackfoot squaw Big Jake took for convenience. She was his safe-passage through hostile Blackfoot territory in the high, rugged forests to the north and west where the Indians called the Rocky Mountains the Backbone of the World, where the Medicine Line marked the Canadian border. Iron Skillet had a vile temper and a sour disposition. She was lazy and troublesome, but she walked out front through bear country. She tended the horses. She pretended to cook. She couldn't sing, but she could hit the high notes when she screeched. She was a source of perverse amusement and uproarious, riotous diversion, a sort of walking, talking, raging conversation piece.

Big Jake could not know that the following summer, of a rendezvous morning, and quite by accident, he would meet a Sioux girl whom he had only to gaze upon for his lonely heart to break, for his head to swoon, for his wild longings to conjure thoughts of long winter nights, of the warmth of a woman, of a mountain cabin and a glowing hearth and strong sons to watch grow, to walk beside him, to fight beside him, to laugh with him and help him string his trap lines. That was before anyone knew the fur trade was coming to an end.

Fair or not, crittur, a man's possessions define him. I'm not saying it's right. It's just how it is. But just worry about possessing the important stuff, crittur—the abstract stuff—the stuff you keep in your heart that's worth getting hanged for. No, I can't explain it any better than that. It's something a man's got to figure out himself.

Sometimes you think you own something, and only years later after you get it all sorted out do you realize it owns you. Sometimes it's that way between a crittur and something he gets to wanting more than he should.

It's less complicated in the world of grammar where possession of most things requires a simple 's. It's that way with most nouns, anyway.

The use of the possessive 's is fine with many inanimate or neutral objects such as, "the law's delay" or "the government's case." However, you are safer using *of* and a following phrase where a possessive noun would strain the sensitivities of your readers.

> Strained: The mountain's top…
> Better: The top of the mountain…
>
> Strained: The building's roof…
> Better: The roof of the building…

Sometimes an adjective expresses ownership better than a possessive noun:

> Avoid writing: The government's regulations…

Instead write: Government regulations…

You do not need the apostrophe before the *s* in the following because they are not necessarily possessive:

> The Writers Club
> The Explorers Club

When more than one person owns the same item—that is, if the one item is owned jointly, or owned in common—list the owners, and place an apostrophe after only the last owner's name.

When more than one person owns more than one item, list the owners, and place an apostrophe after each owner's name.

> The spotted one is Big Jake and Jedediah Smith's horse. (one horse owned by both men)
> Those are Big Jake's and Jedediah Smith's horses. (two or more horses owned separately and individually by both men)

*"Can I Own an Action?" You Ask*
No, crittur, you're not throwing me with this one. Can a crittur own an action? The answer's yes if you're figuring things in a figurative way and no if you get technical. And if you quit smiling long enough and pay attention, you might just learn something here, crittur.

Use a possessive noun or pronoun before a gerund (an action word that ends in *ing* and acts as a noun). The *ing* gerund stops the action of the verb long enough for you to make the action verb into a noun you can own. That's the answer. Ha—you're not smiling now, crittur! (Didn't suppose you would be…)

> Incorrect: Iron Skillet objected to *Big Jake* spittin' and chewin'.
>
> Correct: Iron Skillet objected to *Big Jake's* spittin' and chewin'.

In the incorrect sentence above, we're treating spittin' and chewin' as if they're verbs—which they are not. In the second sentence—the correct one—*spittin'* and *chewin'* are verbal nouns called gerunds and make up the compound object of the preposition *to*. They are preceded by a possessive noun because we want the reader to know who possesses this conduct (spittin' and chewin') that Iron Skillet opposes.

Here's where some grammarians employ a "person distinction" to the equation. They claim both sentences are grammatically correct, but that each has a different meaning. Using the person distinction, the focus of the first sentence is on Big Jake. Iron Skillet objected to Big Jake—the person—who was spitting and chewing tobacco. In the second sentence, Iron Skillet's objection is not to Big Jake, but to his conduct.

Anyway, that's how some grammarians tell it. Still, it is safer to use the possessive, if that is the meaning you are actually conveying. Using the possessive takes the focus off the person or thing doing the action, and places the focus on the action itself.

To be sure you have a gerund and not a verb ending in *ing*, try replacing the word ending in *ing* with a noun. If the noun fits, you have a gerund, and the rule is: Use a possessive noun or pronoun before a gerund. Once you have the noun in place, you can readily see why a possessive noun or pronoun needs to precede it. In the sentences below, when you replace the gerunds *spittin'* and *chewin'* with the noun *obnoxiousness*, you can see why the sentences do not work without the possessive noun or pronoun.

> Incorrect: Iron Skillet objected to *Big Jake* obnoxiousness.
> Incorrect: Iron Skillet objected to *him* obnoxiousness.

> Correct: Iron Skillet objected to *Big Jake's* obnoxiousness.
> Correct: Iron Skillet objected to *his* obnoxiousness.

In the next sentence, when you replace *riding* and *shooting* with the noun *performance*, you can see why the objective pronoun *him* would not work. "Have you seen him performance?" is obviously wrong. All the following sentences need a possessive pronoun or a possessive noun before the gerund.

> Correct: Have you seen his riding and shooting?
> Correct: Have you seen his performance?

Correct: We were concerned about his limping.

Correct: We were concerned about his condition.

Correct: The drunken trappers loved the show. *Big Jake's* catching a bullet in his teeth was funnier than *his* kicking a horse in the butt. The *horse's* kicking back was the best part.

However, if using the possessive gets too cumbersome, you may opt to drop it in favor of the objective case. Just remember, you are on shaky ground without the possessive. The next sentence is technically incorrect, but making the nouns possessive would detract from the flow and flavor of the sentence.

Stinky Petey and Wit-less Winslow spitting chaw into the wind delighted the onlookers.

## *Use Objective Case Pronouns before Participles*

(See Verbals.)

Now listen closely, crittur. The following gets even trickier. We have just said to use a possessive noun or possessive case pronoun before a gerund. Present participles require objective case pronouns rather than possessive case pronouns before them. Hoboy! Let me explain.

In the following sentence, *him* is an objective case pronoun, *shaking* is a present participle.

> The war whoops of the Indians had him
> shaking in his boots.

————◆◆◆◆●————

Iron Skillet was like a snake you hold by the tail. Once you picked her up, it was hard to put her down, and you were never certain exactly how to hold on to her or if you really wanted to. But she was Big Jake's woman now, and theirs was a match conjured in the dark wickedness somewhere between Hades and Hell itself.

But at rendezvous one summer, Big Jake met a longhaired maiden of the Dakota Sioux named Calls Down the Stars. Calls Down the Stars was everything Iron Skillet was not. She was beautiful, shy, and intelligent, and she spoke softly when she spoke at all. Big Jake reckoned those were admirable enough traits in a woman.

————◆◆◆◆●————

## Noun Clauses

Varying sentence structure and length is an excellent way for a writer to achieve a lively, engaging writing style. Toward that end, the noun clause tops the list in an effective writer's arsenal.

A subordinate clause (or dependent clause) contains a subject and verb but does not express a complete thought. A subordinate clause cannot stand alone as a sentence. Some subordinate clauses are noun clauses. A noun clause is a group of words that serves in the sentence where a noun would serve. A noun clause can be used as a subject, direct object, indirect object, predicate noun, or object of a preposition. When you want to add freshness and style to your writing, consider using noun clauses.

> *That I should be good with my fists* never occurred to my challenger. (noun clause as subject)
>
> A detestable little mountain man is *what he called me*. (noun clause as predicate noun)
>
> *A one-two combination to his nose and jaw* settled *the matter in question*. (noun clause as subject and direct object)
>
> At the saloon that night, he told *those who would listen* his detestable little mountain man story. (noun clause as indirect object)
>
> They all sympathized with *whatever he told them* as long as he kept buying them rounds. (noun clause as object of the preposition)

A noun clause often begins with one of the following relative pronouns or subordinating conjunctions: *after, although, as, because, before, how, if, once, since, that, though, those, til, unless, until, what, whatever, when, whenever, where, wherever, which, who, whoever, whom, whomever, whose.* Do not try, however, to determine the kind of clause by the word that introduces it. Noun clauses, adjective clauses, adverb clauses, and Santa Clauses can only be identified by the way they are used in a sentence. (Just wanted to see if you're paying attention, crittur...)

## THE TRUTH ABOUT VERBS

Calls Down the Stars was Sioux and a daughter of the medicine of the night skies. She was young and tall and lithe with the awkward, easy grace of a long-legged filly. Her raven hair and her wide-set eyes were blacker than a starless night.

Her skin was an unblemished, even hue of deep sun-darkened cherry red—her hands, her bare legs and thighs, her face, her throat, her shoulders—the skin of a woman, the stuff of dreams. Big Jake's eyes tried to follow the dark smoothness of her skin as it disappeared beneath the white folds of her doeskin dress. He looked upon her with a longing that ached in the hollow depths of his soul. He looked at her boldly. He looked at her shamelessly and hungrily. He looked at her with all the imaginings of a lonely mountain man.

As the morning breeze played lovingly in her hair, the big man could not take his eyes from her. His feet began to walk toward her, across the blowing prairie grasses, beneath the big sky country of the Yellowstone and the Big Horn, and his eyes saw no one and nothing but her. She saw him coming and she straightened tall and wide-eyed, and when he stopped and stood tall before her in the sunlight and shadows, she was unafraid. He watched her breathing. He watched the rise and fall of her breasts. The man and woman spoke not a word, but his gaze said silently: "My stick floats with yours."

Big Jake was not sure she understood. But he understood. He stood before this dark-eyed Indian girl as his heart pounded in his chest, as the earth stopped on its axis, as the clouds in the sky and the sun above and heaven itself spun in a giddy, heady, dizzying vortex around and around the far horizons. For the first time and forever, Big Jake Mclaughlin was in love.

———◆◆◆◆◆———

Verbs are motion and existence and all that lies between. A noun may be the most magnificent person, place, thing, or idea in the world, but without a verb, that noun can do nothing. Without a verb, that noun cannot even be. Ah, the beauty of it all! Verbs, crittur—I'm talking the coming and the going and the being and the is of all of life and the known universe.

So, let us indulge our fancies in wild and wanton verbishness. What be a verb, crittur? Why a verb be a word that expresses action or a state of being. Hang with me, crittur, I'm getting a little worked up here. Verbs always do that to me. Let's move along now to the innards of verbs and dissect their working parts.

## *Verbs and the Objects They Take*

### *Direct Object*

A transitive verb is an action verb, and a transitive verb takes a direct object. The direct object is the noun or pronoun that receives the action of the verb and answers the question whom or what.

If you have an intransitive verb, no object need apply for the position; the intransitive verb simply links the subject to various predicate parts. In the sentence below, the verb *grew* is intransitive. *Old* and *wise* are adjectives. There is no direct object.

> Silas Potter grew old and wise in the ways
> of the mountains.

You have a direct object when you have a transitive verb.

> Silas Potter taught Big Jake.

Silas Potter taught whom? He taught Big Jake. *Big Jake* is the direct object.

### *Indirect Object*

An indirect object is a noun or pronoun that receives the action of a transitive verb and answers the question *to whom, for whom, to what,* or *for what.* By its very definition, a verb is transitive when it has a direct object. Therefore, you can only have an indirect object when you first have a direct object. Still, an indirect object always comes before a direct object in a sentence.

Silas Potter taught Big Jake sign language.

Silas Potter taught what? He taught sign language. *Sign language* is now the direct object, not Big Jake. He taught sign language to whom? To Big Jake. *Big Jake* now becomes the indirect object.

But watch how things take a wicked grammatical turn when we recast the sentence below.

Silas Potter taught sign language to Big Jake.

*Sign language* is still the direct object, but once you add a preposition—usually *to* or *for*—you have a prepositional phrase instead of an indirect object. In the above sentence, *Big Jake* is the object of the preposition *to*. There is no indirect object.

All right, let's back up and give this some room, crittur. If you're confused, you may be confusing indirect with intransitive. In the first sentence below, *shot* is an intransitive verb because there is no direct object. The preposition *at* comes after the verb. *Parker Daniels* is the object of the preposition, not the object of the verb. In the second sentence, there is no preposition, and *Parker Daniels* is the direct object of the verb.

Locoweed Louie shot at Parker Daniels.
Locoweed Louie shot Parker Daniels.

## The "Be" Verb

"Be" verbs are simply verbs that express a condition of existence or being. With eight forms, the "be" verb is the most irregular of any verb in the American language: *am, is, are, was, were, be, been, being*. But it's worse than that, crittur. You may as well be fearless and add the verb become to the list of "be" verbs. Be fearless, but don't be stupid. Many a mountain man's been shot for ontological orneriness.

| **What a mountain man says:** | **What a mountain man means:** |
|---|---|
| I *be* a mountain man. | I *am* a mountain man. |
| You *be* critturs. | You *are* critturs. |
| Last month, I *be* in the high country trappin' beaver. | Last month, I *was* in the high country trappin' beaver. |
| I *be* trappin' in these mountains for years. | I've *been* trappin' in these mountains for years. |
| We *be* good scouts. | We *were* good scouts. |
| I *be* fearless about grammar. | I *became* fearless about grammar. |

*Using* **Be** *Correctly*

All right—how do we use *be* correctly? Use *be* when you are demanding, requesting, or suggesting something.

Four Flusher Phil found himself captured by a Ree war party. He didn't have much chance against twenty warriors. They tied him to a stake and piled logs and brush at his feet in preparation for a cook-out.

> "I demand I *be* released at once!" Four Flusher Phil told his captors.
> "We request you *be* silent," Red Wing, their leader, told him.
> "I suggest you *be* more civilized," Four Flusher Phil admonished him.
> "No way."
> "Way."
> "Enough talk, paleface!"
> "Wait! I insist I *be* given access to a lawyer!"
> "Good," answered Red Wing. "We cook lawyers, too!"

If you can insert the word "should" before *be*, you are probably using *be* correctly.

> "I demand I *should be* released…"
> "We request you *should be* silent…"
> "I suggest you *should be* more civilized…"
> "I insist I *should be* given a lawyer…"

## *Linking Verbs*

Linking verbs link the subject of a sentence with a noun or adjective in the predicate. That's what the textbooks tell you. But again, be fearless, crittur. Go ahead and link to a predicate pronoun and feel absolutely no remorse about it.

This is it.
I am he.
It was everyone.

Linking verbs do not express action and are not modified by adverbs. Mostly. Now let's take this slowly, crittur. I know you're cute, but cuteness will take you just so far in life and then you'll need mountain man skills to get you through the rough stuff.

To the unsuspecting crittur, the verbs listed below look like "regular" verbs. They are not. They *be* linking verbs. They just *be*—and not a nervous twitch of action do they express—no action whatever. They *be*, they are, they am what they am. Now, it's true, some of these verbs can be action verbs if you get them riled up. That's true of any of us. But follow along, crittur, and trust me on this one. It'll all make sense, I promise.

**Some linking verbs:**
be (am, is, are, was, were, be, been, being, become)
look
seem
feel
smell
taste
grow
appear
sound
remain

*Linking Verbs with Predicate Nouns and Predicate Adjectives*

Linking verbs do just what they say they do—they link the subject of the sentence with a noun, pronoun, or adjective in the predicate. The predicate noun or pronoun renames, defines, or identifies the subject. *Rifle* in the sentence below is linked to the noun *Hawken*, which renames and identifies the subject.

The rifle *is* a Hawken.

The predicate adjective describes the subject. In the example below, the subject *eyes* is linked by the verb *were* to the adjectives *cold* and *glaring*.

His eyes *were* cold and glaring.

In the following sentence, appeared links the subject *Indian* with the predicate adjective *menacing*. *Menacing* describes *Indian*.

The Indian *appeared* menacing.

In the sentence below the subject *rifle* is linked to the adjective *accurate*, which describes the rifle.

The rifle *is* accurate.

In the final sentence, the subject *food* is linked by *was* to the predicate noun *pemmican*. The predicate noun renames, defines, or identifies the subject.

Our food *was* pemmican.

---

In the beginning it was Big Jake's smile that caught the eye of Calls Down the Stars—that wonderful flash of white teeth and the way his eyes smiled honest and guileless and trusting—the eyes of a man who gazed across the dark heavens and saw things beyond a man and a woman in love. As the years passed, Calls Down the Stars of the Dakota Sioux would grow to love Big Jake McLaughlin for his rugged strength, his raw courage, his unbridled generosity, the gentleness of his heart, and the depth of his soul.

Big Jake understood. He understood he had to keep time and distance between that vile Iron Skillet of the Blackfoot and this precious one of the Dakota Sioux named Calls Down the Stars.

---

### *Bad*, *Badly*, *Good*, *and* *Well*

Understanding linking verbs has its practicalities. For one thing, it helps us to use *bad* and *badly* correctly. Okay, crittur, which sentence below is correct?

I felt *bad* about Elmo getting eaten by bears.

**or**

I felt *badly* about Elmo getting eaten by bears.

As used above, *felt* is a linking verb, so a noun or adjective must follow—not an adverb. *Bad* is an adjective, and so the correct answer is "I felt bad." *Badly* is an adverb and adverbs do not modify linking verbs—remember? All right, don't worry about getting this one wrong. In a real emergency, you'd have had me or some other competent coon nearby to help you. Don't be rough on yourself. You're young. You'll change.

Let's try it with an action verb, a linking verb, and a gerund.

> Sarah sang badly. (The adverb *badly* modifies the action verb *sang*.)
>
> Her singing was bad. (The adjective *bad* describes the gerund *singing*. *Singing* is the subject of the sentence.)
>
> I felt bad about her singing. (*Bad* is an adjective describing the subject pronoun *I*. There is no action here, just the being in a bad disposition about her bad singing.)

All right, since you've learned that well, it's well (fitting) we advance to *good* and *well*.

If you were coming down with the grippe, you might say: "I feel ill." *Ill* is an adjective following the linking verb *feel*.

Once you are better, you might say: "I feel well." Here *well* is an adjective meaning healthy. It follows the linking verb *feel*. *Well* is usually an adverb except when it refers to one's health.

When you say: "I am good" you are saying you are well-behaved, or you are good at doing something. "I am well" means you are feeling fine.

> A good writer writes well and feels good about being well.
>> <u>A good writer</u> (*Good* is an adjective describing the noun *writer.*)
>> <u>writes well</u> (*Well* is an adverb modifying the verb *writes.*)
>>> <u>and feels good</u> (*Good* is an adjective following the linking verb *feels.*)
>>>> <u>about being well</u>. (*Well* is an adjective meaning healthy. It describes the verbal *being.*)

*Linking Verbs and Adjectives, Action Verbs, and Adverbs*

As I mentioned before, the same verb at different times can be either an action verb or a linking verb depending on how it is used. Sometimes it gets confusing, but if you can substitute *is* or *was* for the verb, it is probably a linking verb.

*Felt* can be an action verb or a linking verb. It is an action verb in the first example below. In the second example it is a linking verb; it expresses no action on the part of the subject and can be replaced with *was, seemed,* or *appeared.*

> Bill *felt* the beaver fur.
> The fur *felt* soft and smooth.

*Looked* can be an action verb or a linking verb for the same reasons.

Silas Potter *looked* at Jim.
Jim *looked* sad.

### Linking verbs linking with adjectives:

The pemmican *tasted* delicious.

(The linking verb is *tasted*. The predicate adjective *delicious* describes the subject *pemmican*. You can substitute the linking verbs *seemed* or *was* for the linking verb *tasted*.)

The Medicine Man *looked* doubtful.

(The linking verb is *looked*. The predicate adjective *doubtful* describes the subject *Medicine Man*. You could say the Medicine Man was doubtful.)

Big Jake *appeared* angry.

(The linking verb is *appeared*. Big Jake *seemed* angry; he was angry. There is no action here. Not yet.)

Henry and Otis *sound* alarmed.

(Linking verb)

### Action verbs modified by adverbs:

He *tasted* the pemmican eagerly.

(The action verb is *tasted*. The adverb *eagerly* modifies the action verb *tasted*.)

The trapper *looked* up.

(The action verb is *looked*. The adverb *up* modifies the action verb *looked*.)

Big Jake appeared suddenly.

(The action verb is *appeared*. Big Jake came on the scene; he showed up. There is action here. *Suddenly* is the adverb.)

I will *sound* the alarm loudly.

(Action verb)

Remember, adverbs also modify adjectives. In the sentence below, *tasted* is the linking verb, *delicious* is the predicate adjective, and *very* is an adverb modifying the adjective delicious. Not just delicious, but very delicious.

The beaver tail tasted very delicious.

## Helping Verbs (Also Called Auxiliary Verbs) and Verb Phrases

Cute is cute, I don't care who you are. A buffalo-skinner friend of mine is cute. She is especially cute in the way she uses verbs.

That night it rained. Rain, rain, rain, rain, rain—all night long. But the tepee was warm and dry, so we sat inside the tepee and talked. Talk, talk, talk, talk, talk—for hours.

She's cute, all right, and maybe she's just adverb impaired, I don't know. But I think about her when I think about verbs, because verbs work. Work, work, work, work, work. They work so hard, sometimes they need helpers. When they combine with helpers they form verb phrases.

A verb phrase consists of a helping verb and a main verb. Together they are considered one verb.

He *has gone* over the mountain.

Many times a verb phrase will be interrupted by a noun, pronoun, or adverb.

She *is* currently *making* your moccasins.

**Some common helping verbs:**
am, is, are
be, been
was, were
has, have, had
do, does, did
will, shall
can, could
might, may, must
should, would

## *Progressive Verbs, Past and Present*

Now a lesser coon might be tempted to go for a political joke here—progressive, conservative, moderate, liberal, and such. But I shall rise above that. Besides, it wouldn't work anyway. All the political jokes have already been elected.

So, let's get past that and go on to some serious action. The progressive form of a verb expresses action that is ongoing and in progress, continuing from the past. For best results, use the present participle and a form of the verb "be" as a helping verb. In progressive verb forms, the helping verb is the key element for clarity and precision.

> The Kiowa *have been pursuing* me for an embarrassing incident that happened four years ago.

## Verb Tenses

Verb tenses indicate whether an action or circumstance takes place in the past, present, or future. A verb has three fundamental tenses and three perfect tenses. Sometimes the verb changes as the tense changes. Sometimes a helping verb is needed.

| Verb | Past | Present | Future |
|------|------|---------|--------|
| see | saw | I see/ he, she, it sees | will/ shall see |
| look | looked | I look/ he, she, it looks | will/ shall look |
| ride | rode | I ride/ he, she, it rides | will/ shall ride |
| work | worked | I work/ he, she, it works | will/ shall work |

When you want to write or speak of an action or circumstance that was done or existed in a prior time and continued into a later time or continues in the present, you use *perfect tenses*. (Are you following this, crittur?) You form perfect tenses by adding *have, has,* or *had* before the past participle.

Past Perfect (expresses an event or action that took place before another past event or action):

> The mountain man *had thrived* long before the settlers began their westward march.

Present Perfect (expresses an event or action that occurred at a specified or unspecified time in the past and continues into the present):

> Through the years the mountain man *has valued* his independence.

Future Perfect (expresses an event or action that will be completed prior to another event or action in the future):

> I hope the mountain man spirit of independence *will have resurfaced* before our children and grandchildren become too comfortable with modern day government controls.

## Was *and* Were

*Was* and *were* are tricksters. Let's begin by saying they both express a past event or condition. That's the easy part to understand.

> I *was* sure glad to see the cavalry right about then.
> They *were* riding in fast and hard.

But *was* and *were* can be elusive when the mood is subjunctive. You get to say things like "the mood is subjunctive" when the white in your hair and the greasy wood smoke in your lungs and the rancid buffalo jerky in your belly make you mean and wild and revered by younger critturs who can taste the rot o' death on you when they stands too close and swallows hard, and breathes the putrid smell of old bear grease and 'bacca and salted rawhide about you and you stare back at 'em with the crazed hollow-eyed look of an old trapper been too long in the mountains. That's when—and only then—you got the right to say stuff like "the mood is subjunctive." You gettin' this, child? Don't get testy on me now.

*Subjunctive Mood*
Now we'll go through some of the rules, slow and simple, so as not to ruffle your sensibilities. Subjunctive mood, indeed! You pay close attention now, crittur.

Use *were* following "as if" or "as though."

> It seemed as if they *were* not even there.
> He raced as though he *were* running for his
>     life.

Use *were* following "if" when you are indicating something contrary to fact. You may believe it, and it may be true when you say:

> I *was* smarter at trading than the old chief.

But suppose you realize you were cheated in your trading. Once "if" comes into play, *was* becomes *were*.

> If I *were* smarter at trading, I would not
>     have let the old chief make a fool of me.

In the above sentence, you being smarter than the old chief is contrary to fact. But what if you are not sure you were cheated? What if there's a possibility you really were smarter than the old chief? Use *was* if you are not certain whether or not what you are saying is contrary to fact. Use *was*—even after "if"—when there is a question as to the truth or accuracy of an event or condition.

> If I *was* smarter at trading, I never let the old chief know it.
> If I *was* cussin' out loud, at least no one could hear me above the din of battle.

I may or may not have been smarter at trading. I may or may not have been cussin' out loud.

> If Sitting Bull *was* there, no one saw him.

Sitting Bull may or may not have been there.

> If it *was* a genuine Hawken flintlock, it was too rusty to tell.

It may or may not have been a genuine Hawken.

*Wishes and Things Contrary to Fact*
Use *were* when you are expressing a wish or desire.

> I wish I *were* back in camp right now.
> She wishes Stinky Petey *were* a lot better smelling.
> She wishes he *were*n't so stupid.

Use *were* when you are expressing things contrary to fact.

*Were* I you…

I am not you.

If I were rich…

I am not rich.

If Sitting Bull *were* there the fight would have been stopped.

But Sitting Bull was not there to stop the fight.

The word *if* alone does not make the mood subjunctive. Even without the word *if*, you will want to use *were* when you are expressing a condition contrary to fact.

*Were* I as perspicacious as the old chief, I would not have traded a handsome horse for an ugly wife.

Use *was* to express a past event or condition. Use *was* to express a condition not contrary to fact.

I *was* scared yesterday when the battle started.

The above sentence expresses a past condition as well as a true condition—not contrary to fact.

Who *was* leading that war party?

The above sentence expresses a past event as well as a condition of uncertain truth or accuracy.

> I'm not sure, but if it *was* Sitting Bull, he certainly fought like a raging bruin.

Again, the speaker is not certain. It may, or may not have been Sitting Bull. And actually, if Sitting Bull was leading the war party, the speaker would probably not be alive to talk about it.

The following sentence refers to something which may or may not have been a lie:

> If it *was* a lie, I didn't know it at the time.

In this next sentence, no one is owning up to the deed:

> *Was* that you who took that bald guy's scalp a couple years back?

And here, it may or may not have been the spring of '37:

> If it *was* in the spring of '37, I was in the mountains at the time.

Maybe we should end this with a line from Shakespeare's *Julius Caesar*. Mountain men like Shakespeare because there were no established rules of grammar in Shakespeare's time. Ah, Shakespeare— so direct and so complex.

If it were so, it was a grievous fault.

## Would *and* Should

*Would* expresses a wish:

> Would that she were here.
> I would that she were happy.
> I would it were so.

*Would* is used after a wish or some well-intended (or not so well-intended) advice.

> I wish you would quit complaining.

*Would* makes a request.

> Would you leave?

*Would* expresses uncertainty.

> You would think he would learn after all these attempts at making peace with the Comanches.

Finally, *would* softens the harshness of a direct statement.

> That would hardly be honorable, Sagebrush Sam.

*Should* expresses an obligation, a probability, an expectation. Here should means "ought to."

I should smack you in the head, Sagebrush
Sam.

*Should* expresses contingency or possibility.

If you should die at the hands of warring
Indians, Sagebrush Sam, how is anyone
going to believe I didn't kill you first?

*Should* is used in all three (pronoun) persons.

I should say something. We really should
say something.
You should say nothing.
He should go away. They should go away,
too.

Finally, like *would*, *should* softens the harshness
of a direct statement.

Instead of: "I demand an apology."
You may want to say: "I should think you
would apologize."

That's all there is to nouns and verbs at close quar-
ters, and other relationship problems. You're making
good progress, Crittur. I hereby confer upon you the
title of:

## ✴ USUFRUCTUARY OF USAGE ✴

# The Ha'r of the B'ar:

## Mastering the Wily Pronoun

*"A reputation in the morning for meanin' what you say can save you a lot of powder and ball later that evening tryin' t' settle any doubt."*

— SILAS POTTER —

Indian names were descriptive: White Man Runs Him, Standing Wolf, Big Heart, Bruised Head, Iron Legs, Knows His Weapons, Sees the Water, Skunk Comes Out, Man Afraid of His Horses, Big Man, Old Elk, Red Blanket. In the Indian tradition, a name was earned and taken seriously. If you fooled the Crow, your name might be Fools Crow. If you encountered a deer with a bad leg, or such a deer gave you visions in a dream, your name might be Lame Deer.

Once you became an adult, your name was usually with you for life. Big Jake hated his Sioux name, though he had come by it honestly enough. One day a band of Sioux saw Big Jake come riding over the hill with Locoweed Louie at his side. As the two white men rode into the Indian camp, a young brave bellowed in a booming staccato voice, "Here comes Big Man with No Brains!"

Common nouns, proper nouns, and given names can sometimes be cruel, so for this section, crittur, we'll stay with pronouns. Pronouns are kinder. Pronouns don't label. Pronouns don't accuse. Pronouns don't describe. Pronouns just are. Pronouns strip away names and identities and get down to generalities—the essence of what is, what was, and what will be.

## PRONOUNS AND ANTECEDENTS

A pronoun is a word that takes the place of a noun. That's simple enough. But consider that pronouns have antecedents—or should. The antecedent is the noun the pronoun replaces or the noun equivalent to which the pronoun refers. The antecedent may not always be in the same sentence as the pronoun, but it usually precedes the pronoun. In the first example below, the antecedent *rifle* is in the first sentence. In the second example, the antecedent *rifle* comes after the pronoun *it*. The third example demonstrates how the antecedent can even be another pronoun. *Everyone* is the antecedent of the pronoun *his*.

> A rifle was a mountain man's friend. It could
> be counted on in tight situations.
> When it was used as a last resort, the rifle
> was as effective as diplomacy.
> Everyone primed his rifle.

Some grammarians do not agree that every pronoun has an antecedent. They maintain that, strictly speaking, the first person pronouns *I* or *me*, and the third person *you*, do not necessitate an identifiable noun other than some obscure narrator or general reader. The same holds true for the ubiquitous *one* as in: "One is wise to prepare for the unexpected." But that is splitting hairs, as professor types are wont to do. Keep your scalp, and let not your hairs be split or your heart troubled by petty pedantry. Let us just say every pronoun needs an antecedent.

In any case, keep the antecedent clear. When you use a pronoun, your reader needs to understand exactly to whom or to what the pronoun refers. Avoid vague, confusing pronoun construction. In the following sentences, the reader cannot be certain whether the horse or the buffalo snorted—and who found things frustrating, the old mountain man or the kid?

> As he reined his horse up to the buffalo, it
> snorted.
> The old mountain man was teaching the
> green kid how to string a trap line. That
> first week, he found things frustrating.

Using "exacter" nouns clears up the second example.

> That first week, the kid found the lessons frustrating.

## *Pronoun-Antecedent Agreement*

Just as subject and verb must agree in person and number, subject and pronoun must agree in person, number, and gender. You student critturs may recall an English teacher of yours yelling out to his class: "All right—*everyone* take *their* seats!" Well, *everyone* is a singular subject requiring a singular complementary pronoun in the predicate. Change *their* to *his*; change *seats* to *seat*. And while you're at it, change the *English* teacher to an *American* teacher.

> *Each* warrior sat around the campfire telling tales of the scalps *they* took.

*Each* and *warrior* are singular, so the word *they* is incorrect. Change *they* to *he*.

*Agreement in Person*

> A *man* walks out on thin ice, and if *his* luck holds, *you* don't fall through and drown.

The above sentence is incorrect because *his* is a third person pronoun and *you* is a second person pronoun. You need another third person pronoun.

> A *man* walks out on thin ice, and if *his* luck holds, *he* doesn't fall through and drown.

## Agreement in Number

> *Somebody* left *their* whiskey in my possible sack.

The above sentence is incorrect because somebody is a singular subject and their is a plural pronoun. You need a complementary singular pronoun.

> *Somebody* left *his* whiskey in my possible sack.

## Agreement in Gender

In case some of you critturs don't know, gender refers to sex. Not sex sex, but sex. Gender refers to the masculine, feminine, or asexual nature of words. You get the picture. (We mountain men get a bit edgy talking about sex.)

> *masculine*—man, boy, brother, ram, buck
> *feminine*—woman, girl, sister, ewe, doe
> *neuter*—rock, pelt, knife, rifle (unless you call your rifle "Old Gertrude" or some such foolishness)
> *indefinite*—senator, president, lawyer, teacher, offspring, baby, fawn, fold

> As the old grizzly closed in on *its* prey, *he*
> took a devastating swipe with his claws.

The above sentence is incorrect because the neuter pronoun *its* is at odds with the masculine pronoun *he*. Correct the sentence by keeping the gender in agreement throughout.

> As the old grizzly closed in on *its* prey, *it*
> took a devastating swipe with its claws.
> As the old grizzly closed in on *his* prey, *he*
> took a devastating swipe with his claws.

*An Additional Comment on Gender*
His or hers? The pronoun *his* means "mankind" or "all" and refers to both male and female gender. In a gender-mixed crowd of theatergoers or a coed classroom, *his* is correct as a reference to the entire audience or the students in general.

> The audience was delighted. Everyone
> raised *his* voice in a resounding cheer.
> Everyone one in class sat quietly reading
> *his* book.

If a writer is gender sensitive, he (or she) may opt to write:

> Everyone in class sat quietly reading *his or*
> *her* book.

*Pronoun Transfers*

Avoid pronoun transfers. Keep your pronouns consistent. If *mountain man* is the subject of a sentence written in the third person, the subject is ill-served by the second person pronoun *you*.

> If a mountain man needed help from a friend, *you* just had to ask.

Correct the above sentence with a third person pronoun.

> If a mountain man needed help from a friend, *he* just had to ask.

*Two Subjects: Noun and Pronoun*

Do not place a pronoun right after a subject noun. The result is two subjects vying for the same verb.

> The trappers they had a good season.

Correct the above sentence by omitting the pronoun *they*.

> The trappers had a good season.

## NOMINATIVE, OBJECTIVE, AND POSSESSIVE CASE PRONOUNS

Personal pronouns have three cases: nominative case, objective case, and possessive case. Nominative case pronouns (also called subject pronouns) are used as the subject of a sentence. Objective case pronouns (also called object pronouns) are used as the object of a verb or the object of a preposition. Possessive case pronouns show ownership.

The pronouns *it* and *you* may be used as either subjects or objects, but the other personal pronouns belong in one category or the other.

## *Nominative Case Pronouns*

The following are subject pronouns:

|  | Singular | Plural |
|---|---|---|
| First Person | I | we |
| Second Person | you | you |
| Third Person | he, she, it | they |

Nominative case pronouns are used as the subject (or compound subject) of a sentence. *He* and *I* are subject pronouns; *me* and *him* are object pronouns. (See page 117 for a list of object pronouns.) Keep them where they belong.

> He went hunting with me.
> I went hunting with him.
> Me went hunting, too.

The last sentence above is absurd because an object pronoun has no business impersonating the subject of a sentence.

Suppose you are going hunting with Silas Potter. Someone says, "Silas is going hunting." You incorrectly answer:

Me too. Or: Me, too.

You are using an object pronoun (*me*) where the subject should be. Somewhat more correctly, you might say:

I, too.

But here, too, you are not actually correct because your sentence does not have a verb. It is therefore not a complete sentence. At least you are using the proper subject pronoun. To be absolutely correct, you need to say the following:

I, too, shall go hunting.

Too late—Silas left without you.

### The **We** *and* **Us** *Factor*
You know to always use *we* as the subject pronoun and *us* as the object pronoun. The rule applies even when *we* or *us* precedes a noun. When in doubt about *we* or *us*, try saying the sentence to yourself without the noun to hear how it sounds.

> We trappers are an independent breed of men.
> We are an independent breed of men.
>
> We Americans are a patriotic people.
> We are a patriotic people.

He called out to us trappers.
He called out to us.

It didn't take much to give us mountain men
an appetite for straight whiskey and
curvy women.
It didn't take much to give us an appetite for
straight whiskey and curvy women.

### Compound Subject Pronouns

Most critturs have the most problems with most pronouns in most compound applications. Pronouns in
compound subjects can be confusing. Know your
subject pronouns and your object pronouns, and
keep them in their proper places. The following sentences are dead wrong.

Incorrect: Molly and me went hunting.
Incorrect: Her and I hobbled the horses and
made camp.

In the first sentence above, *me* is an object pronoun and is never used as the subject of a sentence.
You need a subject pronoun *I*. "Molly and I went hunting." If you drop Molly from the first sentence, you
cannot say: "Me went hunting." Well, you could if you
wanted to, but then please don't ever tell anyone you
read this book.

In the second sentence *her* is an object pronoun
and is never used as the subject of a sentence. You
need a subject pronoun here. "She and I hobbled the
horses and made camp." If you drop the *I* from the

second sentence, you cannot say: "Her hobbled the horses and made camp." Her did, yes, indeed. (Hoboy!)

In a compound subject always put the *I* or *we* last. It's good manners, crittur. All of the following sentences are correct.

> Reverend Blake and I never saw eye to eye.
> Reverend Blake and we never seemed to agree on anything.
> Reverend Blake and we trappers held different views on whiskey and women.

In most sentence constructions, the noun or pronoun in the subject comes before the verb. But the subject is not always a noun or pronoun and the verb sometimes comes first. When the verb comes before the pronoun, be especially careful to use the subject pronoun.

> "You got that right, hoss," answered he.
> Down the steep embankment fell she.

Use the subject pronoun after the linking verb *be*. Remember the "be" verbs: *am, is, are, was, were, be, been, being, become*.

> It is I.
> Woe is I. (as Patricia T. O'Conner so aptly says in her book of the same title.)
> The winner of the foot race was he.
> The winners of the battle were they.

When it comes to pronouns following "be" verbs, many clean-cut, low-mileage grammarians favor a common, folksy approach. As a mountain man, I disagree. Read on, crittur.

Suppose Judge Donahue asks you, "And would the man who tried to bushwhack you be in this very courtroom, Mr. Crittur?"

You answer, "Yes, your honor."

"And would you be inclined, Mr. Crittur, to be pointing out that very man?" asks Donahue.

Now think a minute, crittur. Although most modern day grammarians would tell you it is perfectly all right to answer, "Yes, that's him, your honor," you had better remember your rules of grammar. Always use a subject pronoun after a "be" verb.

"Yes, that's he, your honor," is the only grammar you should utter—and so you do.

Upon hearing you speak with such a facile command of grammar, Donahue may ask, "Mr. Crittur—don't you know the queen's English?"

You answer loudly and proudly, "Yes, your honor, I have heard she is."

And upon knocking on a door and being asked to identify himself, a timid crittur may in confidence affirm, "It's me." But not the gentle reader crittur. The gentle reader crittur is not timid. The gentle reader crittur knows about the "be" verb and the subject pronoun following it. A crittur is never ashamed to be heard speaking proper American grammar.

Knock! Knock!

"Who's there?"

"It is I, the gentle reader crittur!"

Though it may be lost on some folks, notice below how Cactus Charlie's correct grammar gives others the impression that Cactus Charlie is a man of intelligence and elegance.

> "Cactus Charlie," asks Nathan, "be that thar the medicine man what last evening sold you the bad whiskey what almost killed you?"
>
> "I do believe it's he, Nathan, yes."
>
> "And, Cactus Charlie, be that thar the unfortunate lookin' squaw you earnestly married last night when you was in the throes of not seein' straight and too overcome with love to pronounce yer own name?"
>
> "Woe is I, Nathan—woe is I!"
>
> "Be that her—that unfortunate lookin' one?"
>
> "Yes, that's she, I do believe, Nathan."
>
> "I knowed you'd remember soon's yer head cleared, Cactus Charlie. 'Cause no one could never fool you, no sir. Yer right smart—ceptin' you talks real funny, Cactus Charlie—right funny peculiar, you does."

## *Object Pronouns*

Objective case pronouns are either direct or indirect objects, or objects of prepositions. Be sure to use objective case pronouns where objects are needed.

Here is a list of objective case personal pronouns:

|  | Singular | Plural |
|---|---|---|
| First Person | me | us |
| Second Person | you | you |
| Third Person | him, her, it | them |

The following examples are a tad long, but they are comprehensive. If the gentle reader can get through them and understand them, he's well on his way to mastering some of the wiliest of all the pronouns—the objective case pronouns. Let's give this a go, crittur.

> The scout warned Captain Kruger and *him* of an imminent Indian attack.

Here *him* is part of a compound direct object.

> They sounded the alarm for Bravo Company and *us*.

*Us* is part of a compound object of the preposition.

> Let *us* get something straight between *us*.

The first *us* is the direct object. The second *us* is the object of the preposition *between*. *You* is the implied subject of this sentence.

> Let *us* get something straight between *you* and *me*.

This sentence is almost the same as the preceding sentence. *Us* is the direct object. *You* and *me* are compound objects of the preposition *between*. *You* is the implied subject of this sentence.

> A score of *us* trappers led the charge.

*Us* is in apposition with *trappers* and the object of the preposition *of.*

(See Appositives and Prepositions.)

> Seeing Big Jake there, Stinky Petey was so happy, he hugged *him.*

*Him* is the direct object. *Him* receives the action of the verb *hugged.*

> Big Jake gave *him* a powerful warning about public displays of affection.

*Him* is the indirect object. *Him* indirectly receives the action of the verb *gave.*

> Still, folks got to talking about *them* being alone too long in the mountains.

*Them* is the object of the preposition *about.*

### Compound Object Pronouns

Take special notice of the pronouns in compound objects. Many critturs have many problems with many pronouns in many compound applications. It would be simple enough if most critturs would most times mostly remember to not use a subject pronoun as the object of a verb.

> He went hunting with Bill and I.

The above sentence is incorrect. *I* is a subject pronoun. You need an object pronoun here. He went hunting with whom? He went hunting with *me* not *I*.

He went hunting with Bill and *me*.

The following sentences are correct. The subject nouns and pronouns are underlined. The object nouns and pronouns are italicized:

> <u>Wit-less Winslow</u> and <u>I</u> went hunting with *them*.
> <u>They</u> went hunting with *Wit-less* and *me*.
> <u>They</u> went hunting with *us*.
> <u>Jake</u> and <u>they</u> went hunting.
> <u>He</u> and <u>they</u> went hunting.
> <u>They</u> went hunting with *them*.
> <u>Jake</u> and <u>I</u> met *Wit-less Winslow* and *him*.
> <u>Wit-less Winslow</u> and <u>he</u> met *Jake* and *me*.

In a compound object, always put the *me* or *us* last. It's good manners.

> <u>He</u> shot at *Wit-less Winslow* and *me*.
> <u>They</u> shot their arrows at *Reverend Blake* and *us*.
> <u>They</u> tried to kill *Reverend Blake* and *us trappers*.

Never use a reflexive or intensive pronoun as the subject of a sentence. Never use an intensive pronoun as the object of a verb. You may use a reflexive pronoun as the object of a verb or the object of a preposition, but do not substitute a reflexive pronoun for a legitimate object pronoun. (See the section on Reflexive and Intensive Pronouns. Go ahead, crittur, do it now.)

## Possessive Case Pronouns

Possessive pronouns indicate ownership or possession. Do not use an apostrophe with a possessive pronoun to indicate possession. There are two kinds of possessive pronouns. One kind you use before a noun; the other is used alone:

### USE BEFORE A NOUN:

|  | Singular | Plural |
|---|---|---|
| First Person | my | our |
| Second Person | your | your |
| Third Person | his, her, its | their |

### USE ALONE:

|  | Singular | Plural |
|---|---|---|
| First Person | mine | ours |
| Second Person | yours | yours |
| Third Person | his, hers, its | theirs |

It's *my* flintlock.
The flintlock is *mine*.
It's gonna be *your* scalp, Big Jake.
The scalp they take will be *yours*, Big Jake.

## PROBLEM PRONOUNS AND THE VERBS WHO LOVE THEM

In this section on problem pronouns, you'll find a lot of pronouns assuming titles: demonstrative, reflexive, intensive, relative, interrogative, indefinite, and all manner of fancy handles. Be not troubled. You can do this, crittur. You probably already know a lot about these pronouns; you just were never formally introduced. So, allow me to introduce to you my pronoun friends.

### *Indefinite Pronouns*

An indefinite pronoun does not refer to any particular person, place, thing, or idea. An indefinite pronoun does not specifically identify, refer to, or name its antecedent. Indefinite pronouns can cause confusion as to number (singular or plural). Let's start with singular indefinite pronouns first.

*Singular Indefinite Pronouns*
These indefinite pronouns are always singular:

> another, anyone, anybody, anything, each,
> either, everyone, everybody, everything,
> much, neither, no one, nobody, one,
> nothing, someone, somebody, something

Of the singular indefinite pronouns, *anyone, anybody, everyone, everybody, no one, nobody, someone, somebody, each, either,* and *neither* seem to cause the most problems as to number. Generally, they are singular personal pronouns, and when coupled with personal possessive pronouns or reflexive pronouns, they require singular elements throughout the sentence. But remember, crittur, there are exceptions to many grammar rules.

All the sentences below begin with singular indefinite pronouns as their subjects. The incorrect sentences begin with the singular subject and finish off with the plural possessive pronoun *their* or the plural reflexive pronoun *themselves*. The sentences need singular pronouns throughout. The sentences have been corrected by replacing the plural pronouns with singular pronouns to complement the singular subjects.

> Incorrect: Everyone get *their* own gun.
> Correct: Everyone get *his* own gun.

> Incorrect: Has anyone found *their* bullets?
> Correct: Has anyone found *his* bullets?

> Incorrect: Each have *their* own method of trapping beaver.
> Correct: Each has *his* own method of trapping beaver.

> Incorrect: No one envisioned *themselves* as heroic in the face of two thousand enemy warriors.
> Correct: No one envisioned *himself* as heroic in the face of two thousand enemy warriors.

Be careful when a phrase or other words come between the pronoun and the verb.

In the sentence below, the subject is the singular pronoun *everything*, so the verb needs to be singular. *About mountain men and Indians* is a prepositional phrase with a compound object.

> *Everything* about mountain men and Indians is interesting.

In the following sentence, *each* is the singular subject pronoun. It requires a singular verb (*was*) even though the object of the preposition is plural (*trappers*).

> *Each* of the trappers was inclined to take an Indian wife.

Be careful of the pronoun *each* when you place it before a prepositional phrase. Generally, when a sentence begins with the pronoun *each*, the verb and all other complementary elements must be singular. But when each follows a plural subject or compound subject joined by *and*, the verb and all other complementary elements must be plural. That's because, in that construction, *each* is not a pronoun; it is an adverb. An adverb is never the subject of sentence.

> Each of the trappers has his own method of trapping. (Each has...)
> The trappers each have their own methods of trapping. (Trappers have...)

Other times the pronoun *each* is not a pronoun or an adverb, but an adjective. An adjective is never the subject of a sentence, and so the dynamics change again.

> Each Crow man and boy brag openly of their horse stealing.

In the above sentence, *each* is an adjective. Man and boy are elements of a compound subject joined by *and*. The sentence requires the plural verb *brag*. In the sentence below, *each* is a pronoun and the subject of the sentence. *Each* is a singular subject and requires the singular verb *brags*.

> Each brags openly of his horse stealing.

---

The Crow Indians dearly loved the land they called Absaroka, the land of the Sparrow Hawk People. In the heat of the summer they thrived in the high, cool mountain pastures; in the unforgiving winter they snuggled warm in their winter camps along the wooded rivers below or in the beautiful Wind River valley. It was all Crow land, all of it good horse country with good water and abundant game.

The mountain man, too, loved the Crow land. He loved its proximity to the rolling prairies where the buffalo and antelope were plentiful, and its high forests of elk and deer. The white man especially loved its creeks and streams with their abundance of plews.

And especially, too, he loved the land of the Sparrow Hawk People for the unabashed, uninhibited, openly promiscuous company of the Crow women.

The Crow were good-natured and friendly. Their men were handsome and intelligent. They loved willing women, droll humor, laughter, wild tales, and cheerful camaraderie. Their women were not unattractive, though not beautiful in any classic, noble sense. Still, the women were shamelessly amorous and inordinately attracted to visiting white men. They smiled freely and flirted shamelessly with the mountain men.

The Crow were carefree, happy thieves. The men and boys bragged openly about their horse stealing, and the mountain men respected them for their truthfulness.

The Crow genuinely liked the white man. They had no overwhelming desire to kill the whites, burn them out, or drive them off the land. Why should they want to drive away the whites who brought with them horses to steal?

———◆◦◆◦◆◦◆———

*Plural Indefinite Pronouns*
These indefinite pronouns are always plural:

both, few, many, others, several

The pronoun *both* gets special attention. *Both* needs balance. A careful crittur must balance adjectives (especially articles), adverbs, prepositions, and verbs equally in the *both* equation. The first sentence below is incorrect. If the article *a* precedes *cheat*, the same article should precede *liar*. We've corrected that in the second sentence by balancing the both equation with another article.

> Incorrect: Parker Daniels was both *a* cheat and liar.
> Correct: Parker Daniels was both *a* cheat and *a* liar.

The following sentences are balanced; they either have balanced articles or none at all. Either way, it was well a crittur knew: Parker Daniels was an equal opportunity scoundrel.

> Parker Daniels lied both to the red man and to the white man.
> Parker Daniels lied to both red man and white man.
> His conniving both angered and frustrated the trappers.
> His conniving was both infuriating and frustrating.
> He had both a cold heart and a devious mind.
> He stole both ruthlessly and indiscriminately.

Do not use *both* with *as well as*.

> Incorrect: Parker Daniels carried both a gun as well as a knife.

Correct: Parker Daniels carried both a gun
and a knife.

Correct: Parker Daniels carried a gun as
well as a knife.

Some grammarians hold that *all of, both of, each of, some of*, etc., should be followed by a pronoun. Well, maybe. The sentence below appears sound enough without following pronouns.

*All of* pride and honor were at stake.

But there is something to be said for the use of fewer words. Taking this rule farther, deeper, and wider than many grammarians, I say drop the *of* and fearlessly follow *all, both, each, some*, etc. with not just a pronoun, but, indeed, a noun, adjective (especially article), adverb, or almost anything your little black heart desires. Hence:

*All* pride and honor were at stake.

At Rendezvous, some mountain men gambled away *all* their pelts and *all* their money.

## Singular or Plural Indefinite Pronouns

Now listen, crittur, just when you start to believe you've mastered the singular and plural indefinite pronouns, things have a way of getting dicey. The following indefinite pronouns are either singular or plural depending on the antecedent to which they refer:

all, any, more, most, none, some

Contrary to popular belief, and contrary to the way television news anchors use the pronoun, *none* can mean *not one* (singular) or *not any* (plural). But in her book *Woe is I*, Patricia T. O'Conner maintains, and I concur, that *none* has always been closer in meaning to the plural *not any* and that it requires a plural verb.

Still, too, *none* can be singular when it refers to a singular entity as in *not any of it, no part of it, not one element of it.*

*None* of the powder was dry enough to fire.

In the above sentence, *none* means *no part of,* no amount of the powder was dry enough. Here *none* is singular and takes a singular verb *was.* But the jury is still out on this one, crittur, and so we live with the mix of meanings and usage.

> None is willing to leave the mountains. (Not one is willing—singular verb)
> None are willing to leave the mountains. (Not any are willing—plural verb)
> None of Stinky Petey's wives have been known to fight over him. (Not any have—plural verb)
> None of the horses were shod. (Not any were—plural verb)

Perhaps if the writer really wants to indicate "not one horse" he should write it that way.

Not one of the horses was shod. (Not one was—singular verb)

The pronoun *all* has problems all its own. When you use *all*, you must know whether the pronoun represents or takes the place of a singular noun or a plural noun. One must consider the entire context of what is being said or written. This is particularly true when the indefinite pronoun is the subject of a sentence and the verb must agree with it.

That is all…

Those are all…

All the mountain men are gone. (All of them are…plural verb)

All their glory is gone. (The one sum total of their glory is…singular verb)

All he knows is what life in the mountains has taught him. (The one sum total of what he knows is…singular verb)

All the old traditions are lost. (All of those old traditions are….plural verb)

(See All, Any, None and Subject-Verb Agreement.)

### *Either* and *Neither*

*Either* and *neither* try to be all things to all critturs. They can take singular or plural verbs depending on the components of the sentence. *Either* and *neither* can be adjectives, conjunctions, or, pronouns; and *either* can be an adverb.

*Either* and *neither* as conjunctions:

Neither Seth nor Matt can handle a buffalo
rifle very well.

Seth can't shoot, and neither can Matt.

Either fish or cut bait.

*Either* and *neither* as adjectives:

Neither one is competent.

Shoot at either buffalo.

*Either* and *neither* as pronouns:

Neither is likely to survive alone in the
mountains.

Either will do nicely.

*Either* can be an adverb meaning *also* or *too*.

He is not trusting of government agents,
and I'm not either.

As pronouns, *either* and *neither* (when *neither*
means *not either*) are usually used with a singular verb.

Either is a competent guide. (They are both
competent.)

Neither is a competent guide. (They are
both incompetent.)

### *Either-or* and *Neither-nor*

When you use *either-or* or *neither-nor* with singular
entities, use a singular verb.

Neither the size nor the color is right.

When you use *either-or* or *neither-nor* with plural entities, use a plural verb.

> Either bullets or arrows are effective on horse thieves.
>
> Neither words nor bullets are going to persuade him.

When you use *either-or* or *neither-nor* with a mix of singular and plural entities in the same sentence, the entity closest to the verb determines whether the verb is singular or plural.

> Neither Jim nor the Indians are willing to settle the dispute.
>
> Neither the Indians nor Jim is willing to settle the dispute.
>
> Either the land is wild or the Indians are not.

*Either-or* and *neither-nor* have other requirements. Both sides of the equation must be balanced and complementary. Whatever grammatical entity comes after *either* must also come after *or*. Whatever grammatical entity comes after *neither* must also come after *nor*. If your sentence has a subject-verb after *either*, you need a subject-verb after *or*. If a preposition follows *either*, a preposition must follow *or*. Verb must complement verb; adjective must complement adjective, etc., to balance the sentence.

The following sentences are correctly balanced:

> Either Stinky Petey goes, or I go. (subject-verb complements subject-verb)
>
> Big Jake is either in hiding or in jail. (prepositional phrase complements prepositional phrase)
>
> Soft-Headed Sylvester is neither sober nor trustworthy. (predicate adjective complements predicate adjective)
>
> Locoweed Louie neither aims right nor shoots straight. (verb-adverb complements verb-adverb)

The following sentences are out of balance:

> Either Big Jake wins or loses. (Imbalance: subject-verb, verb)
>
> Correct it this way: Big Jake either wins or loses. (verb, verb)
>
> Neither Stinky Petey is here nor Big Jake. (Imbalance: subject-verb, verb)
>
> Correct it this way: Neither Stinky Petey nor Big Jake is here. (subject, subject)

The same balance is required for *not only...but also*, and *both...and*.

> Balanced: A trapper had to contend not only with hostile Indians, but also with angry grizzlies.

Out of Balance: A trapper had to contend not only with hostile Indians, but also angry grizzlies.

Another way to correct the sentence is to move *with* out from the middle of the equation. Thus, the following is correct:

A trapper had to contend with not only hostile Indians, but also angry grizzlies.

## Demonstrative Pronouns

A demonstrative pronoun indicates a specific but unnamed noun.

*This* is great!
*That* was awful.

*This* and *that* are singular; *these* and *those* are plural. *This* and *that* suggests a distinction between one thing and another. *These* and *those* suggests a distinction between two or more things and two or more other things. *This* makes reference to the person or thing close at hand, nearby, or just mentioned.

This is my squaw.

*This* can indicate something is about to be said.

Hear this...
Listen to this...

Sometimes *this* and *that* make for a difficult choice. In general reference, *that* is preferred by grammarians. Having said that, there is a rule to keep at the ready. Generally, *that* refers to a prior occurrence—that which has happened.

> The knife had blood on it. That in itself was enough to shift suspicion to Sagebrush Sam.
>
> That was wonderful!

When the reference is yet to be made, *this* is used in reference to future occurrence—what is about to be said:

> This is what I know…
> This is what I believe…

Also, in informal writing and speech, *this* is sometimes used as an emphatic substitute for an uninspired, indefinite article. But in formal writing, avoid using *this* to replace *a* or *an*, as shown:

> I have this nagging worry about an Indian attack when we least expect it.

The next sentence answers the above sentence using *this* in reference to a future event:

> This is how to solve that—expect an attack at any time!

*This* (here it comes, this thing in the future
I'm about to say) is how to solve *that*
(the thing in the past of which we are, or
have been, speaking)—expect an attack
at any time!

*This* and *these* are used to indicate things that are close.

This is the place.
These are mine.

*That* and *those* are used to indicate things at a distance.

That is over on the other side of the creek.
Those are there, too.

In the following narrative, see how the pronoun *this* can be a subject or an object. At the end of the story, Big Jake uses *this* as the subject of a sentence. The Indian uses *this* as the object of the verb *take*.

Big Jake came through the trees silently and
unseen to the edge of the creek. He hid
there in the shadows and watched as
Sagebrush Sam waded the creek to set his
beaver traps. Big Jake smiled to himself at
his unexpected good fortune. Then, moving silently, stealthily through the brush,
Big Jake worked his way upstream to a
thicket of willows around the wide bend

of the creek. There, upstream of Sagebrush Sam, the big man stripped down. Wearing only his moccasins and a smile, Big Jake quietly entered the water where, in the cool flow of the middle of the creek, he did the exceedingly nasty thing all little kids do in pools, lakes, and bathtubs. He smiled perfidiously, luxuriating in the long, warm, and satisfying nature of his act. His smile lingered as the warmed water flowed downstream toward Sagebrush Sam.

"*This* is for you, Sagebrush Sam," he thought wickedly.

Upstream of both men, around the next bend of the creek, an Indian waded into the water. Smiling, the red man, too, luxuriated in his own long, warm, and satisfying act.

"Take *this*, Paleface," he thought wickedly.

*This* and *that*, *these* and *those* are perfectly respectable demonstrative pronouns, but they moonlight as demonstrative adjectives.

Below *this* is an adjective describing *book*. *Book* is the subject of the sentence.

*This* book is informative.

In the following sentences, *this*, *these*, *that*, and *those* are demonstrative adjectives.

*This* saddle and *these* two loaded scatterguns are mine, Honest Joe.

*That* saddle is yours, Honest Joe, but it's on
my horse—and so are you.

*That* mule is yours, Honest Joe, but *those*
pelts on its back are mine.

Listen here, Honest Joe, *those* expressions
on your face of shock and innocence
don't make no never mind to *these* two
loaded scatterguns.

## *Reflexive Pronouns and Intensive Pronouns*

Reflexive and intensive pronouns end with *self* or
*selves*. A reflexive pronoun is a pronoun that
directs the action of the verb back to the subject of
the sentence. An intensive pronoun is a reflexive
pronoun that intensifies or adds emphasis to the
noun or pronoun already named. Not that you
would ever really have to make the distinction—
except maybe in an American grammar class—but
there is an easy way to tell a reflexive pronoun from
an intensive pronoun. If the real meaning of the
sentence cannot be conveyed without the pronoun,
it is most likely a reflexive pronoun. If the real
meaning of the sentence can be conveyed without
the pronoun, the pronoun is most likely an intensive pronoun.

| **Singular Reflexive and Intensive Pronouns** | **Plural Reflexive and Intensive Pronouns** |
|---|---|
| myself, yourself herself, himself itself | ourselves, yourselves, themselves |

Reflexive pronouns direct the action of the verb back to the subject. The reflexive pronoun is necessary for a full understanding of the sentence.

> Stinky Petey never seemed concerned about *himself*. (reflexive pronoun as object of the preposition)
> He never bathed *himself*. (reflexive pronoun as direct object)
> He never bought *himself* any soap. (reflexive pronoun as indirect object)
> Big Jake reminded *himself* to keep his powder dry. (reflexive pronoun as direct object)

Intensive pronouns intensify or add emphasis to the noun or pronoun already named. The intensive pronoun may be omitted and the reader can still understand the full meaning of the sentence. An intensive pronoun is never the subject of a sentence or object of a verb or preposition.

> Big Jake checked the gunpowder *himself*.
> Chief Running Bare *himself* wanted the pleasure of taking Big Jake's scalp.

> The chief dreamed of doing the honors
> *himself.*
>
> I *myself* have considered it.

Young critturs in particular should remember: Never use *hisself* for *himself.* Never use *theirselves* for *themselves.* *Hisself* and *theirselves* are not legal words anywhere west of the Mississippi River. In plain, young-crittur American: There are no such words as *hisself* and *theirselves.* They don't exist. Please tell the young ones never to use them.

Never use a reflexive or intensive pronoun as the subject of a sentence. Never use an intensive pronoun as the object of a verb. You may use a reflexive pronoun as the object of a verb or the object of a preposition, but do not substitute a reflexive pronoun for a legitimate object pronoun.

In the following sentences, the reflexive pronouns are correctly used. *Myself* is correctly the direct object of the action verb *hit.* *Himself* is correctly the object of the preposition *about.*

> I accidentally hit myself in the head with
> an ax.
>
> He never talked much about himself.

But the following sentences need to be corrected. In the first sentence, *me* would be the correct object pronoun, not *myself.* In the next three sentences, *me* and *us*, not *myself* and *ourselves*, would correctly be the objects of the prepositions *like*, *with*, and *among* respectively.

Incorrect: The raiding war party tried to kill
  Big Jake and myself.

Correct: The raiding war party tried to kill
  Big Jake and me.

Incorrect: That was too much to bear for a
  sensitive guy like myself.

Correct: That was too much to bear for a
  sensitive guy like me.

Incorrect: Ned and myself went hunting
  buffalo. Big Jake went with Ned and
  myself.

Correct: Ned and I went hunting buffalo.
  Big Jake went with Ned and me.

Incorrect: The buffalo meat was divided
  among ourselves.

Correct: The buffalo meat was divided
  among us.

## Relative Pronouns

A relative pronoun is a pronoun that relates back to a
noun as it connects a subordinate clause to a main
clause. *Who, whom, whose, that,* and *which* are relative pronouns. In the following sentence, *that* refers
back to and relates to *dog.*

Big Jake had a dog that hated him.

Below, the relative pronoun *who* refers back to
and relates to *crittur:*

A crittur who was there saw Big Jake get sucker-punched in a saloon and bit by his own dog when he was knocked to the floor.

In the next sentence, the first *that* refers back to and relates to *trousers*; the second *that* refers back to and relates to *bite marks*; the third *that* refers back to and relates to *knuckle-nubs*:

Big Jake had trousers that were ripped, bite marks that decorated his butt, and knuckle-nubs that graced his skull.

Depending upon the antecedent, *who, which*, and *that* can be singular or plural.

The trappers who were there…
The trapper who was there…
A trap which was later set proved effective…
The traps which were later set proved effective…
The beavers that were trapped…
The beaver that was trapped…

Now things get a little tricky again. City folks might call it "ambiguity," but it's plain tricky when other words come between the relative pronoun and its antecedent. The following sentence needs the singular verb *understands* because the pronoun *who* refers to the antecedent *one*, a singular pronoun:

> A mountain man is one who *understands*
> the wilderness.

The sentence is absolutely correct. (As absolute as grammarians will venture…) But just to bedevil us and tax our acumen, grammarian Jan Venolia, and probably Patricia T. O'Conner, may put forward the question: What if we insert the words *of those*? Now we have a slightly different sentence:

> A mountain man is one of those who *understand* the wilderness.

Why does the singular verb *understands* now become the plural verb *understand*? Most grammarians will answer that *one* is no longer the antecedent of the pronoun *who*. *Those* (the object of the preposition) is now the antecedent. *Those* is plural, and so a plural verb is correct.

> Incorrect: Parker Daniels is one of those slimy
> gamblers who is not welcome in camp.
> Correct: Parker Daniels is one of those slimy
> gamblers who are not welcome in camp.

The same logic applies to the pronouns *that* and *which*.

> Incorrect: An early freeze is one of the
> things that worries a trapper.
> Correct: An early freeze is one of the things
> that worry a trapper.

Incorrect: One of the questions which troubles all of us concerns his competence.
Correct: One of the questions which trouble all of us concerns his competence.

### *That* and *Which*

We are now at the ever dangerous *that* versus *which* end of the pronoun pony. Choosing between them can bedevil even veteran grammarians. But choices are easy when you're fearless—mindful that fearlessness can kill a man who doesn't know the way the stick floats. So, let's break this down into something that looks like logic.

*Which* can be restrictive or nonrestrictive. When *which* is a nonrestrictive pronoun, it heralds in a parenthetical clause not essential to the sentence and should be set off with commas. When *which* is a restrictive pronoun and introduces a clause essential to the sentence, no comma is needed.

The first sentence below tells where the rifle is located and adds information that is nonessential to the meaning of the sentence. The second sentence tells where one may find a specific rifle in need of cleaning.

The flintlock, which needs cleaning, is lying on the ground.
The flintlock that needs cleaning is lying on the ground.

*Which* can be restrictive or nonrestrictive. *Which* can be a pronoun or an adjective.

Which horse shall we steal? (adjective, restrictive)

This horse, which I stole from a Blackfoot brave, is the best horse I've ever owned. (pronoun, nonrestrictive)

Of course, you could make the last sentence restrictive and omit *which*—if that construction expresses your meaning:

This horse I stole from a Blackfoot brave is the best horse I've ever owned.

Nevermind, crittur, what some grammar books tell you about using *which* only to introduce a nonrestrictive clause. *Which* is versatile, fearless, even reckless at times:

…travel which way you will…

…during which time I managed to escape with my life.

The lure which called me to the mountains…

*That* can be a subject or an object.

That is my Flintlock! (subject)

He wore that in public! (object)

*That* can be an adverb.

It doesn't take that much effort to be unreasonable.

He was that fast.

*That* can serve as a conjunction.

> That George Armstrong Custer will live on
> in legend is certain.
> That he will lie to save his hide is a safe bet.
> He was a bad Injun, that's for sure.
> That Iron Skillet was not to be fooled with
> was well-established.

*That* is effective when used elliptically.

> That idiot!
> Joker that he was.

*That* can be a pronoun or an adjective.

> That's right. (pronoun)
> That knife is sharpest. (adjective)

*That* can denote who, whom, or which.

> The horse that the Indians shot out from
> under him was just as much a soldier as
> he was (a soldier).

*That* can indicate when.

> It was the year that Sitting Bull died.

*That* can express a wish or strong emotion.

> Oh, that Sitting Bull were still alive.
> Would that I were there at the last rendezvous.

*That* can be the antecedent for *which*.

> A season of beaver plews was only a fraction of that which I gambled away.

*That* serves a myriad of functions and when used correctly can invigorate your writing.

> This is horse poop, and that is shinola!

### Choosing **That** or **Which**

*Which* is used in reference to animals and inanimate objects. *Which* should never be used to refer to people. Use *who* when referring to people. It is becoming ever more acceptable to use *that* in reference to people, but the old mountain men *who* (not *that*) cling to the old ways believe who is cleaner, clearer, politer.

> The man *who* shot me was a whiskey running varmint named Parker Daniels.

Choosing *that* or *which* is not always easy. Consider the following sentences about medicine. Each sentence is correct depending on whether or not your reader knew from previous text that the medicine was made from snake venom.

> The medicine which he concocted from
> snake venom almost killed me.
> The medicine that he concocted from snake
> venom almost killed me.

In both sentences, *that* and *which* are restrictive. That means they are not introducing parenthetical information. They are introducing information necessary for understanding the sentence, and therefore, they are not set off with commas. The first sentence declares that it was the snake venom in the medicine that almost did him in. The second sentence uses the snake venom to identify the medicine, but blames the medicine itself for the near fatality. The medicine was just bad stuff.

There's an old saying among mountain men when things get confusing, or when they think they're being lied to. They'll look a man in the eye and say: "It sounds pretty good—if you say it fast enough." So, I'm going to say the following really slooowly:

Most times you can simply omit *that* or *which*. If you can omit *which* and still keep your intended meaning, you could have used *that* instead of *which* to begin with. If using *that* rather than *which* does not change your meaning, it is usually better not to use either one.

> The medicine he concocted from snake
> venom almost killed me.

All right, we got that out of the way. Pay attention, crittur, there's more. If you are still not sure whether to use *that* or *which*, use *that* and do not set off the clause with commas, or simply omit *that*.

> If given a choice, the Bowie knife was the
> weapon that most fighting men preferred.
> If given a choice, the Bowie knife was the
> weapon most fighting men preferred.

*Which* and *that* can be singular or plural depending upon the usage.

> Which one *runs* the fastest? (singular verb)
> Which ones *run* the fastest? (plural verb)
> He chose the path that *was* wrong. (singular
> verb)
> He chose the paths that *were* wrong. (plural
> verb)

### *Who* and *That*

You know now that *that* and *which* are used to refer to animals and inanimate objects. You know *that* is sometimes used in reference to people, but *who* is always preferable. Know also, crittur, to use *who* when referring to cherished pets with names.

> The horse that threw me…
> The snake that bit me…
> Poor little Fifi, who from the depths of her
> little doggie heart believed she could
> scare off a grizzly bear with her little
> bark…

*Who* can be restrictive or nonrestrictive.

> That thieving yellow-bellied snake who ran off with our horses was my best friend. (restrictive)
>
> That thieving yellow-bellied snake, who was my best friend, ran off with our horses. (nonrestrictive)

## Interrogative Pronouns

An interrogative pronoun asks a question. *Who, whom, whose, which*, and *what* are interrogative pronouns.

> What is your name, paleface?
>
> Which is my share of the victuals?

*Who* is a subject pronoun (nominative case). *Whom* is an object pronoun (objective case)

> Who asked for your 'pinion, Big Jake? (*who* is the subject)
>
> Whom do you seek, paleface liar? (*whom* is the object of *do seek*)
>
> For whom is this pemmican? (*whom* is the object of the preposition *for*)

*Whose* is a possessive pronoun, but it assumes varied functions. *Whose* can be an adjective describing a noun:

> Whose scalp is that hanging from your belt? (*whose* describes or modifies *scalp*)

*Whose* can stand alone as the subject of a sentence:

Whose was better?

*Whose* can stand alone as a direct object:

Whose did you steal this time, Big Jake?
(*whose* is the object of *did steal*)

### Who's *and* Whose

Be particularly careful of *whose* and *who's*. I've seen this one trip up even careful writers. It makes you look a little foolish when it's wrong and when it's been wrong for a long time because it's been posted on a memo or message (or wanted poster) for all your friends and cohorts to see. And your name's on it and no one tells you it's wrong and silly, until a couple of weeks later you notice it yourself. Not that it's ever happened to anyone I know personally...

*Whose* is a possessive pronoun. Possessive pronouns do not have apostrophes. *Who's* is a contraction meaning *who is* or *who has*. The word *who's* needs an apostrophe.

Whose Green River knife is this? (possessive pronoun)
Who's got my knife? (who has...)
Who's the cook in this outfit? (who is...)

*Who, whose, which,* and *what* can be singular or plural depending upon the usage.

Who *is* there with you, Injun scout? (singular verb)

Who *are* you, paleface? (plural verb)

Whose *is* this? (singular verb)

Whose *are* those? (plural verb)

Which rifle *shoots* center? (singular verb)

Which rifles *shoot* center? (plural verb)

He is swearing to what *appears* to be a lie. (singular verb)

He is swearing to what *appear* to be lies. (plural verb)

When using *what* with two verbs in the same sentence, keep the verbs in the same tense. The second sentence below is correct. The first is not.

Incorrect: What *determines* a mountain man's success is his cunning and his daring. (singular verbs)

Correct: What *determine* a mountain man's success are his cunning and his daring. (plural verbs)

The first sentence is incorrect because *cunning* and *daring* should be treated as two entities requiring a plural verb. It sounds good, however, because we did not mix up the verb tenses. Good verbs cover up a multitude of mistakes.

## Other Problem Pronouns

### It's *and* Its

This one isn't as tricky as it looks. *It's* is a contraction meaning *it is* or *it has*. *Its* is a possessive pronoun. Remember, possessive pronouns never have apostrophes. Let us pretend we are watching a dog eat dog food. We might say, "It's eating its food."

> It's trapping season in the Rockies. (it is…)
> It's been snowing all day in Donner Pass. (it has…)
> Its food is mule meat. (possessive pronoun)

### You're *and* Your

This, too, is as easy as riding a wild buffalo into camp so your woman could cook it up, maybe skin it in the process.

*You're* is a contraction meaning *you are*. *Your* or *yours* are possessive pronouns. Remember, crittur, possessive pronouns do not have apostrophes.

> You're getting on my nerves, Locoweed Louie. (you are…)
> Your socks should be washed in the creek, not in the stew pot. (possessive pronoun)

### Them *and* Those

*Them* is an objective case pronoun. Never use *them* as the subject of a sentence. Never use *them* as an adjective to describe a noun or pronoun.

Incorrect: We saw them buffalo on the horizon.

Correct: We saw them on the horizon.

Correct: We saw the buffalo on the horizon.

Incorrect: I caught them horse thieves red-handed.

Correct: I caught them red-handed.

Correct: I caught the horse thieves red-handed.

*Those* is an adjective when it is followed by a noun. *Those* is a pronoun when it stands alone.

Those buffalo stampeded through my camp. (adjective)

Those are the ones that almost killed me. (pronoun)

That's the long and the short of pronouns, crittur. Congratulations. I hereby confer upon you the title of:

### ✳ PROTECTOR OF THE PRONOUN ✳

# LOADING YOUR PACKHORSE:

## Moody Verbs and More of the Advanced Stuff

*"Strength, power, wisdom, even good fortune, all come from the purity and courage within a man's heart, the determination within his mind, and the quickness of his wits."*

—SILAS POTTER—

A man receives nothing but his life from the Great Spirit. After that, the Great Spirit just watches silently. He gives nothing more. Strength, power, wisdom, even good fortune, all come from the purity and courage within a man's heart, the determination within his mind, and the quickness of his wits.

> "The Blackfoot warriors pray to the Creator for
> success in stealing the horses of the Crow. The
> Crow hunters pray to the Creator for a success-
> ful hunt and for protection for themselves and
> their horses. Will the medicine of the Blackfeet
> be stronger than the medicine of the Crow? The
> Great Spirit watches to find out."

>                                          ⌐SILAS POTTER

Moods were a complication for a man as simple as
Big Jake McLaughlin. There were moody horses and
moody mules. The Indians were moody about their
land. Trappers could get moody about what they
called their territory. A man could get real touchy
about you borrowing his horse without asking. Or his
woman, to a lesser extent. Women? Women were just
moody by nature, especially come courtin' time. And
for some men, courtin' time was all the time.

But Big Jake was different on that score. Big Jake
liked his women to come to him, or so it seemed to
Iron Skillet. There were some days she'd search for
hours before she found him.

## MOODY VERBS

Verbs have three moods. That's a lot fewer than the
moods of a woman. When a woman gets moody, a
man's got trouble. And when a woman can back up
her mood with some irrefutable facts that put her in
that mood in the first place, a man ain't got a prayer—
and no amount of 'splainin' is ever going to make that
bend in the river run straight.

Someday, crittur, I'm going to write another book called *The Mountain Man's Field Guide to Taming Women—How to Avoid Gettin' Your Underwear Washed, Hung, and Ironed While You're Still Wearin' 'Em*. I'm going to write that book as soon as I put a little time and a lot of miles between me and a certain "little woman" in my life. We'll leave it at that, crittur. For now, let's just get back to grammar and pleasant reveries.

There are just three verb moods: indicative, imperative, and subjunctive.

| Mood: | Function: | |
|-------|-----------|---|
| *Indicative*: | States a fact or asks a direct question. | He is a mountain man, all right. (he is) |
| | | Does he usually smell this bad? (he does) |
| *Imperative*: | Issues a command or request. | Take a bath, Stinky Petey. |
| *Subjunctive*: | States a condition contrary to fact or issues a recommendation. | If I were he, I would take a bath or go away. |
| | | I suggest he take a bath or go away. |
| | | I suggest he go away and take a bath. |

## The Verb Got

(*got*: past, past participle of *get*)

Grammarians will tell you, you've got to avoid *got*. I say, maybe. It's true, there are more accurate words to use in its place (*was, have,* etc.), but *got* has its own charm, especially when spoken by charming characters, and especially for intensive sentence construction.

All right, let us play around with *got*. In the sentence below, *got* should be replaced with *understood*.

> He read it over twice before he *got* it.
> He read it over twice before he *understood* it.

Sometimes it is best to eliminate *got* or replace it with a more accurate word.

> Got has got its own charm.
> Got has its own charm.
> Every time the weather got cold and damp,
>      he got the miseries.
> Every time the weather *was* cold and damp,
>      he *contracted* the miseries.
> Every time the weather *became* cold and
>      damp, he *caught* the miseries.

But I still prefer the sentence with the two *gots*. It's got a punch to it. And for intensive construction, nothing beats:

> As Big Jake laughed, the beans got snorted
>      out of his nostrils.

You just cannot write "the beans were snorted" and capture the same imagery. Actually you would want to recast this sentence into an active voice. You should also omit the comma and the word *of* so the reader gets the entire imagery all at once:

> As Big Jake laughed he snorted beans out his nostrils.

Hey—you *got* to love it!

## VERBS RAISING THEIR VOICES

Verbs are cast in either an active voice or a passive voice. Verbs have an active voice if the subject is doing the action. Verbs have a passive voice if the subject is receiving the action or not personally performing the action. Generally, good writers try to write in an active voice. An active voice lends crispness to your writing.

> His *horse kicked* Big Jake in the head. (active)
>
> *Big Jake was kicked* in the head by his horse. (passive)
>
> *Big Jake picked* himself off the ground, holding his head, but smiling and exulting. (active)
>
> His whiskey bottle in his coat pocket *was unbroken*. (passive)

The passive voice works well when the action acted upon is more relevant than the person or thing doing the action, or when the specifics of the subject are vague.

> A powwow was called.
>
> The secret was out in the open now.

———◆•◆◆•◆———

Big Jake had a reputation for fearlessness, if not foolhardiness. But Big Jake was wise and skillful in the ways of the wilderness. He was resourceful. He was trustworthy.

It was Big Jake with whom Jedediah Smith partnered up that winter to cross the Popo Agie River and the continental divide of the Wind River Mountains. It was never established exactly where Jed Smith had first encountered Big Jake, but it was General William Ashley who had advised Smith to search for recruits "in grog shops and other sinks of degradation."

February found them moving through winter snow along the foot of the Wind River Mountains. The snow kept them from crossing the mountains through a high pass, so they decided to cross farther south through a gap near the Popo Agie.

The buffalo and elk had moved to the lower country where the snow was not as deep covering the grass. By the first of March the men had not eaten for four days. It was impossible to start a fire. It was so cold the flint stuck fast to the skin and ripped at it as the flint was pulled away. The men attempted to fire their rifles into dry tinder. All efforts to get a fire going proved unsuccessful. It was just too cold.

———◆◆◆◆◆———

The last sentence above is grammatically incorrect because the thought is incomplete. *Too cold for what?* (See **to, too, two**.) But, the sentence conveys a mood, the reader knows exactly what I mean, and I like it well the way it is, thank you.

## TRANSITIVE AND INTRANSITIVE VERBS

A transitive verb is an action verb that takes a direct object. An intransitive verb is a verb that does not take a direct object. Some verbs cannot stand alone without an object, others can. Some verbs can be either transitive or intransitive.

*Bought* is a transitive verb and needs a direct object. You cannot say:

He bought.

*He bought* makes no sense. If a crittur said that to you, the gentle reader, your first response would be: "Bought what?" Your second response would be an intense, unspoken dislike for the unfortunate crittur. The crittur needs to supply the verb with an object.

He bought…(*what?*)…a horse.

But *laughed* and *smiled* are intransitive verbs. Intransitive verbs make perfect sense without a direct object. You can simply say:

He laughed.
or
She smiled.

Some verbs can be either transitive or intransitive:

She *sang.* (intransitive)
She *sang* a song. (transitive)
He *called.* (intransitive)
He *called* to me. (still intransitive—*to me* is a prepositional phrase, not a direct object)
He *called* me. (transitive)
She *read* his book. (transitive)
She *read* about Africa. (intransitive—*about Africa* is a prepositional phrase, not a direct object)

The next time you look up an unfamiliar verb in the dictionary, check to see whether it's transitive or intransitive. The dictionary will tell you. Knowing what kind of verb it is will help you to use it correctly.

Now, you're getting the hang of this, crittur. Sweet. I hereby confer upon you the title of:

★ **VIRTUOSO OF VERBS** ★

# COUNTING COUP:

Modifying and
Modulating with
Adjectives and Adverbs

*"It doesn't take fancy words
to call a man a liar, a cheat,
or a horse thief."*

⟩SILAS POTTER⟨

Big Jake was a storyteller, valued on long, cold, and lonely winter nights around a fireside. The fact that he had a penchant for stretching the truth and modifying reality only added to his charm.

Once when Bill Sublette was discussing firemaking, knife-sharpening, tracking, and woodsman's skills in general, it was Big Jake who casually mentioned the need to always carry a sharp knife. "Back on the Yellowstone, in the old days—the wild days—I would sharpen my knife so often, why, after a while it got so thin it only had one side to it."

Another time Wiley Willie commented on what a big bruiser of a son of a cock-eyed, low-life she-bear Big Jake was. "You sure is a outsized crittur," Wiley Willy says with genuine admiration and a defensive smile, just in case.

"And it be a sorry disadvantage, too, if you want to know the Gawd's honorest truth," says Big Jake. "Why, I'm so tall," says Big Jake, "that when I'm up trappin' in them thar high mountains, yonder, there be times I'm obliged to duck my head and crouch down low just to let the sun go by."

Big Jake seemed not the least gratified that, right about here in his account, his audience of grungy coons marveled in more than one gap-toothed smile. No, Big Jake continued unhumbled. "Why I'm so tall, I has to climb a ladder just to put on my hat." More smiles, more gaps, fewer teeth at that one.

But Big Jake was undeterred by size when the conversation shifted to travels in hostile Indian territory. "When I'm in the country of the Ree or Blackfeet, I get around safe enough by stealth and skilliness," he said. *Skilliness* was a word Big Jake had made up hisself and he liked it well enough, for sure. "Why, in hostile territory, I make myself so small, it would take seven braves, two squaws, and a dog to see me."

Yes, Big Jake could modify reality. Which brings us circuriously to adjectives and adverbs. Adjectives and adverbs are modifiers. They describe and modify other words—change, hone, fine-tune, and moderate. But unlike Big Jake, they do not stretch the truth, they make the truth more exact.

An adjective is a word that describes a noun or pronoun. An adverb is a word that modifies a verb, an adjective, or another adverb. Adverbs only modify action verbs, not linking verbs.

In understanding adjectives and adverbs, it is important to understand the difference between *describe* and *modify*. Technically, both adjectives and adverbs are "modifiers" and are referenced as such by grammarians. Modifiers make the meaning of words more precise. Adjectives do that by *describing* nouns and pronouns. They tell about nouns and pronouns: what color, what size, what kind, which ones, how many, etc. Adverbs modify verbs, adjectives, and other adverbs. Adverbs change the meaning of the words they modify by telling where, to what extent, how powerful, how ineffectual, how many, how often, and any other tattle-tale gossip they can impart.

## ADVERBS

An adverb is a word that modifies (changes the meaning of) a verb, an adjective, or another adverb. Adverbs fine-tune the meaning of the words they modify. You may say, "I *ran*." But when you say, "I ran *slowly*," or "I ran *quickly*," the adverb indicates a more accurate account of how you ran. An adverb typically expresses time, place, manner, to what extent or degree, etc.

He rode his horse well.

The adverb *well* gives a more precise meaning to the verb *rode*. We could have said, "He rode his horse *badly*," or "He rode his horse *awkwardly*." The verb *rode* alone does not tell the reader as much as the verb and adverb together.

But in the next two sentences, the adverb modifies an adjective. The adverb *very* modifies and changes the meaning of the adjective *tall*. The adverb *bright* changes the meaning of the adjective *yellow*.

> He was a very tall coon.
> The Indian woman wove a bright yellow blanket.

In the following sentence, the adverb *very* changes the meaning of the adverb *bright*. Here you have an adverb modifying another adverb. *Very* changes the meaning of *bright*, which changes the meaning of the adjective *yellow*, which describes the noun *blanket*.

> The Indian woman wove a very bright yellow blanket.

In the next examples an adverb modifies a verb, and an adverb modifies another adverb.

> He stalked slowly.
> He stalked very slowly.

The adverb *slowly* fine-tunes, or changes the meaning of the verb *stalked*. How did he stalk? He stalked slowly. Then the adverb *very* fine-tunes, or changes the meaning of another adverb *slowly*. How slowly did he stalk? He stalked very slowly. Are you following this, crittur?

## *Effective Use of Adverbs*

Contrary to the views of sedentary grammarians gathering dust on their horizontal surfaces, it is permissible to stuff an adverb between a helping verb and main verb. In the following sentence, the helping verb *would* and the main verb *tell* are split by the adverb *certainly*.

He would certainly tell her when he saw her.

Adverbs can be placed almost anywhere in the sentence when they modify action verbs.

The wolf stalked *quietly* through the trees.
The wolf *quietly* stalked through the trees.
Through the trees the wolf *quietly* stalked.
*Quietly* the wolf stalked through the trees.

But be careful when the adverb modifies an adjective or another adverb. In some cases, by changing where the adverb is placed in the sentence, the sentence meaning can be drastically altered. The following sentences are all grammatically correct, but they say entirely different things:

The cannon fire hit nearly all of us. (Many people were injured.)

The cannon fire nearly hit all of us. (No one was injured. It was a close call.)

She punched only one drunken mountain man. (One mountain man was punched by her. All the other mountain men were spared her wrath.)

She only punched one drunken mountain man. (She kicked and bit all the others.)

(See Mutant Modifiers.)

So, while it is true that an adverb may be placed almost anywhere in a sentence, logic should rule. And there are some guidelines. Generally, an adverb should be positioned as close as possible to the word it modifies, and preferably before the word it modifies. Interrogative sentences skew the equation a tad, but old-fashioned horse sense prevails in the end.

(Ever wonder, young crittur, why logic and horse sense are so often spoken of as "old-fashioned"?)

Incorrect: It almost was comical watching Big Jake run from Iron Skillet.

Correct: It was almost comical watching Big Jake run from Iron Skillet.

Incorrect: Do you ever recall agreeing to that?

Correct: Do you recall ever agreeing to that?

Placing your adverb in the beginning of your sentence can add punch to your writing. But in many cases, your adverb makes its most emphatic appearance in between your helping verb and your main verb.

> *Resolutely*, Iron Skillet vowed Big Jake would be a domesticated and devoted husband.
>
> *Ironically*, Iron Skillet's vows held true when Big Jake ran off and married another squaw.
>
> Big Jake was *clearly lucky* Iron Skillet was a bad shot with a rifle. He *would forever* thank whatever gods may be that the old squaw was as blind as she was evil.

**"You can't always keep your powder dry, so always keep your knife sharp and handy for those days of high water and close encounters."**

⌒**Silas Potter**

## *Adverbs, Comparatively Speaking*

As do adjectives, some adverbs compare. When adverbs compare they take two forms, comparative and superlative. Comparative adverbs compare two things, one to the other. One horse may run faster than another horse. Superlative adverbs compare three or more things. Another horse may run the fastest of all the others.

| Adverbs | Comparative | Superlative |
| --- | --- | --- |
| swiftly | more swiftly | most swiftly |
| | less swiftly | least swiftly |
| skillfully | more skillfully | most skillfully |
| | less skillfully | least skillfully |
| frequently | more frequently | most frequently |
| | less frequently | least frequently |

Parker Daniels bathes *frequently*.

Big Jake bathes *more frequently* than Stinky Petey. (comparative)

Big Jake's horse bathes *more frequently* than Big Jake. (comparative)

Of all of them, the camp dog bathes *most frequently*. (superlative)

Some adverbs take irregular form and become a different word in the comparative and superlative.

| Adverbs | Comparative | Superlative |
| --- | --- | --- |
| well | better | best |
| much | more | most |

(See Adjectives, Comparatively Speaking.)

## *Preposition or Adverb?*

A preposition is a word that relates a noun or pronoun to other words in a sentence. A prepositional phrase begins with a preposition and ends with a noun or pronoun, or something pretending to be a noun or pronoun—like a noun clause. The noun or pronoun (or noun clause) is the object of the preposition.

A preposition is a cowardly varmint. It never stands by itself against the world. It's always accompanied by an object. If there is no following object, the word is not a preposition, it is probably an adverb.

Unlike a timid preposition, an adverb stands up boldly and announces itself. But depending on how it is used in a sentence, a word can be either a preposition or an adverb.

> He rode *along*. (*Along* is an adverb modifying the verb *rode*.)
>
> He rode *along the river*. (*Along* is a preposition—*along the river* is a prepositional phrase.)

> Bullets whizzed *past*. (Here there is no preposition or prepositional phrase. *Past* is an adverb modifying the verb *whizzed*.)
>
> Bullets whizzed *past his head*. (*Past* is the preposition followed by the object of the preposition *head*. *Past his head* is the prepositional phrase.)

> His horse was sheltered *inside*. (*Inside* is an adverb modifying the verb was *sheltered*.)
>
> His horse was sheltered *inside the barn*. (*Inside* is a preposition and *inside the barn* is the prepositional phrase.)

"Words ain't proof, and words ain't gonna back you up. So, if you take a stand, be ready to get it on alone. Keep your eyes open, keep your knife sharp, and keep your back to the cliff wall. If you must fight, be fearless and quick, and once committed, for better or worse, never waver. You do all that, and if you're lucky, you may just fight your way out all right. Either way, win or lose, you'll leave your mark on the earth. That's all a man knows and all a man can ever have. And that's enough. Tonight's pipe by the campfire is promised to no man."

⌐SILAS POTTER

## ADJECTIVES

An adjective is a word that describes a noun or pronoun. Adjectives tell what color, what size, what kind, how many, which one, and that kind of stuff. And be careful, 'cause a man can get himself hanged for the wrong adjective, that's for certain.

> Defendant: "He come into my camp in the middle of the night, yer honor. But I wasn't scared. Ain't no little runt gonna scare me. I shot him dead."
>
> Judge: "Guilty! If yer wasn't scared—if he was so little, anyway—why in tarnation did you have to shoot him?"

See what I mean, crittur, about adjectives gettin' a man hanged? Now, consider this next scenario, take a lesson from it, and store it safely in the recesses of your mind.

> Defendant: "He come into my camp in the middle of the night, yer honor. I was scared out of my mind. I shot him dead."
>
> Judge: "Not guilty! Why in tarnation was he sneaking around in the middle of the night anyway? Must o' been up to no good."

Many adjectives come before the noun they describe.

> The *old* trapper died. (The adjective *old* describes the noun *trapper.*)
>
> The *lazy* sentinel slept under the tree. (The adjective *lazy* describes the noun *sentinel.*)

For emphasis, try placing the adjective after the noun it describes.

> The divorcee, *wild* and *carefree,* was out on the town.
>
> The Indians, *proud, fearless,* and *noble* came riding into our camp.
>
> ...hair *long* and *blonde*
>
> ...eyes *cold* and *glaring*

Adjectives that describe pronouns usually come after the pronoun and the linking verb. In the following sentences, the adjective *exhausted* describes the personal pronoun *we*; the adjective *better* describes the personal possessive pronoun *theirs*.

> When we finally reached the fort, we were exhausted.
> Big Jake knew theirs was better.

## Adjectives and the Comma Problem

If adjectives describe, they need to describe accurately. Commas help them do that. Use a comma between two or more adjectives that equally describe the same noun. Do not use a comma when the adjective is a number or when the adjective designates many or few. Do not put a comma between an adjective and the noun it describes.

All right, let's try this out. The rule says do not use a comma when the adjective is a number or when the adjective designates many or few. So, in the next sentences, no comma sets off the number *two* or the word *many*.

> Two wet dogs fought over a bone.
> Many laughing Indians gathered to watch them.

But consider the sentence below.

> We had three cold, blustery winter months.

The rule tells us, no comma goes after the number *three*. But why is there a comma after *cold* and no comma between *blustery* and *winter*? The rule says, use a comma between two or more adjectives that equally describe the same noun. Well, don't *blustery* and *winter* equally describe *months*? To find out for sure, let's try interchanging the adjectives.

*Interchanging Adjectives*

If you are not sure whether two adjectives equally describe the same noun, reverse the order of the adjectives by interchanging them. If the adjectives are equal, the sentence will make sense even with the adjectives reversed. Only if the adjectives are equal do you need to place commas between them.

> Original sentence: We had three cold, blus-
> tery winter months.
> Reversed adjectives: We had three blustery,
> cold winter months.

It seems the comma is needed here because *cold* and *blustery* describe equally. But *winter*, too, is an adjective describing the noun *months*. Let's again reverse the order of the adjectives.

> Original sentence: We had three cold, blus-
> tery winter months.
> Reversed adjectives: We had three cold,
> winter blustery months.
> Reversed adjectives: We had three blustery,
> winter cold months.

Here the reversed adjectives do not work. Only the adjectives *cold* and *blustery* equally describe *months*. They are interchangeable, so a comma is needed between them. But neither one can be interchanged with *winter*. *Winter* needs no comma to set it off from the other adjectives. Consider the next sentence.

> He was chewing on tough buffalo jerky.
> Original sentence: He was chewing on tough buffalo jerky.
> Reversed adjectives: He was chewing on buffalo tough jerky.

Here reversing the adjectives doesn't work. The adjectives *tough* and *buffalo* do not equally describe *jerky*; hence, no comma goes between them. But mountain men are known to bend the rules as far as they can, and they don't always see things the way grammarians do. Any mountain man with any common sense quickly recognizes that, in the above sentence, *tough* is describing *buffalo jerky* as one entity—an adjective describing both the next adjective and the noun together. Now, that may be a sneaky, cheating, easy way to see this thing, and grammatically unsound, but we're mountain men, and that's the way it makes sense to us.

So, crittur, if you can kind of scrunch things up in your mind and see the adjective as describing both the next adjective and the noun, you do not use the comma. In other words, do not use a comma if the second adjective is an integral part of the noun it describes. Let's test this twisted thinking and see if it leads us on a straight course.

There is a difference between the following two sentences. Both adjectives, *young* and *courageous*, may or may not equally describe the *trapper*, but, clearly, the second sentence describes him more accurately as a complete entity. In the second sentence, no comma is needed.

> He is a young, courageous trapper. (*Young* and *courageous* describe *trapper*.)
>
> He is a courageous young trapper. (*Courageous* describes *young trapper*— an adjective-noun considered together as integral parts of one entity.)

And in the following sentences, *soiled* describes *old buckskins*. *Vacuous* describes *blue eyes*. You get the picture.

> He wore soiled old buckskins.
> She had vacuous blue eyes.

Consider the Stinky Petey problem below.

> Stinky Petey was a little, ornery fellow.
> Stinky Petey was an ornery little fellow.

We'll give up the first sentence to all the bow-tied grammarians sitting behind their desks. In the first sentence above, the adjectives *little* and *ornery* equally describe the noun *fellow*. In our second sentence we have the adjective *ornery* describing the *little fellow*, the two words taken as integral parts of one entity. The sentences mean different things, and if you did not have the comma in the first sentence, a reader might think Stinky Petey was only a "little ornery" or a "slightly ornery" fellow.

### The **And** Factor

If you are not sure whether two adjectives describe the same noun, try putting the conjunction *and* between them. You are safe using a comma in the place where *and* fits nicely and completes the sentence logically.

> That day we had a dozen new, accurate rifles.
> That day we had a dozen new and accurate
>      rifles.

In the sentence below, neither *and* nor a comma should go between *new* and *saddle*.

> He bought a new leather saddle.

## Adjective-Noun Agreement

Adjectives must agree in number with the nouns or pronouns they describe. Be particularly careful with *this*, *that*, *these*, and *those*. Understand that *this* and *that* are singular adjectives. *These* and *those* are plural adjectives. Use the proper verb to complement them. (Refer to Demonstrative Adjectives.)

Do not use *kind of, sort of, type of* except in their literal sense. Use *rather* to mean: on the contrary, instead, more accurately, more precisely, more preferably, somewhat, or to a certain extent.

> It was rather scary seeing Iron Skillet on her wedding night.

(See Rather.)

## *Types of Adjectives*

Not all adjectives describe in the same manner. Some are more mannered than others.

### *Proper Adjectives*

Proper nouns become proper adjectives when suffixes are added to make them describe nouns or pronouns. Proper adjectives are always capitalized. As a general rule, do not capitalize compass directions unless they are specific geographic locations, such as the American West.

> Russia becomes Russian as in Russian Roulette.
> America becomes American as in American frontier.

### *Indefinite Adjectives*

Indefinite adjectives do not specify an exact amount or a specific quality.

> *Some* mountain men took *more* precautions than others. *Many* mountain men took *fewer* chances and were less at risk.

(See **less** vs **few**.)

*Demonstrative Adjectives*

In grammar, the word *demonstrative* indicates a link or a reference to another entity. *This, these, that,* or *those* are demonstrative adjectives when they describe or refer to specific nouns that follow. In sentences where they stand alone—where they do not precede a noun—they are demonstrative pronouns.

As pronouns, *this, that, these,* and *those* take the place of specific persons, places, things, or ideas. As adjectives, *this* and *that* describe singular nouns; *these* and *those* describe plural nouns.

| In close proximity or nearby | Farther away or at a distance |
|---|---|
| ...*this* horse... | ...*that* squaw.... |
| ...*these* pelts... | ...*those* traps... |

| Demonstrative Pronouns | Demonstrative Adjectives |
|---|---|
| *This* is great. | I love *this* rum. |
| I heard *that.* | Did you hear *that* sound? |
| *These* are great shelters. | *These* nights are cold. |
| *Those* were good times. | *Those* times were the best. |

Use this and that with the singular nouns *kind, sort,* and *type.* Use *these* and *those* with the plural nouns *kinds, sorts,* and *types.*

> Incorrect: How dangerous are *these* kind of snow storm?

Correct: How dangerous is *this* kind of snow storm?

Correct: How dangerous are *these* kinds of snow storms?

Correct: He was *that* type of hombre.

Correct: *That* sort of shelter will not be adequate.

Correct: The wind howls through *these* kinds of trees.

Correct: Don't go worrying about *those* types of myths.

Correct: *These* kinds of stories always spook lonely men around a winter campfire.

Never use *here* or *there* with demonstrative adjectives.

Incorrect: I shot that there buffalo.

Correct: I shot that buffalo.

———◆◗◆◖◆———

The Indian loved the spotted or "painted" horse, perhaps because of its natural camouflage. And perhaps to drive fear into the hearts of their enemies, some plains tribes bred their spotted war horses to have black hooves. As the Indian butchered and ate or traded away his solid colored horses, the spotted horse became his calling card. Even years after the wild Indians had been subdued and left to rot in misery on reservations, the white man still harbored a prejudice against the pinto and skewbald horses that reminded him of the old days and the old ways of the red man.

The Spanish conquistadors may have brought the pinto to the American West, but the Nez Perce Indians bred the famed Appaloosa, which they prized above all other breeds. The Appaloosa took its name from the Palouse River region of Idaho and Washington—the original range of the Nez Perce. The Nez Perce were accomplished, careful horse breeders and their Appaloosa stock had a look of virile nobility. Though not a big horse, it was hearty and rugged and capable of surviving on what the wild, unforgiving mountains and prairies had to offer. The Appaloosa could do anything a rider asked of it, from high jumps, to speed, to sure-footed endurance and stamina.

As the red man's preeminence diminished with each mile of the white man's westward progress, the stock of spotted and skewbald horses the Indians favored grew weaker. The Indian had not been circumspect in breeding his horseflesh. The warriors and the hunters had preferred the best of the spirited stallions—the "buffalo runners"— which they kept staked to their lodges. The lesser horses were left to graze freely and breed with the mares. The result was a breed of sad looking Indian ponies the cowboys derisively called cayuses or Indian horses. But, by then, the Indians had all been defeated and subdued. With their rich culture destroyed, their spiritualism in shambles, the red man was herded safely onto reservations where mission schools, whiskey, and unemployment erased any remnants of his culture, and the Jesuits crushed into the dust whatever was left of his language and religion. In the end, the red western sun set finally and forever on the free, wild Indian and his noble spotted horse.

---

## *Articles*

There are only three articles: *a, an, the.* And maybe a lot of folks don't think of articles as adjectives. But an article is an adjective in the same unsuspecting way a preacher's daughter can blush behind her wedding veil, or a mountain man can don his best elk skins and be a gentleman, or a loaded scattergun can keep the peace at a wedding between the two.

*A* and *an* are indefinite articles modifying an indefinite, unspecified noun or pronoun. *The* is a definite article denoting a particular noun or pronoun.

> He stole *a* horse. (any one of the horses)
> It was *an* Appaloosa. (any one of the Appaloosa horses)
> He got as far as *the* river before they shot him. (the reference is to one specific river)

### *Using Articles Wisely*

When you use articles, use them carefully. Use articles in repetition to designate separate and individual persons or items. Using articles carelessly can impart an unintended meaning. Consider the following articles in repetition:

> The trapper and the guide arrived at dawn.
> (Here we are talking about two men, one of them a trapper, and one of them a guide. They both arrived at dawn.)
>
> The trapper and guide arrived at dawn. (Here we are talking about one man who is both a trapper and a guide. He arrived at dawn.)
>
> He sold the horse and the saddle. (The horse and the saddle were sold separately in two separate sales.)
>
> He sold the horse and saddle. (He sold the horse and saddle together as one sale for one sale price.)
>
> Sagebrush Sam stole a brown and a white horse. (He stole two horses, one brown, one white.)
>
> Sagebrush Sam stole a brown and white horse. (He stole one horse of brown and white coloration.)

When nouns in repetition refer to the same person or thing, the indefinite article is not repeated.

> Kit Carson earned a reputation as an Indian Scout and guide.
>
> Big Jake was a trapper, hunter, tracker, and guide. He was a mountain man.

Definite articles may be repeated for style, effect, emphasis, and to make your point decisively.

> George Armstrong Custer thought of himself as the judge, the jury, and the executioner.

*Vowels, Vowel Sounds, and Articles*

Vowels are certain letters of the alphabet. The vowels are: *a, e, i, o, u* and sometimes *y* when the *y* sounds like *i* or *e*—as in "sky" or "technology." The rest of the letters of the alphabet are consonants. Vowels need to concern us when they are the first letter of certain words. Consonants need particular attention when they are the first letter of certain words and they take vowel sounds. So, what are the rules?

The basic rule: Write or say the article *an* before most vowel sounds. Notice I didn't say use *an* before most *vowels*; I said *vowel sounds*. Even though the word *one* begins with a vowel, you would not say, "It was *an* one time opportunity." That's because *one* does not have a vowel sound. It sounds like "won"— beginning with a *w*.

You could correctly say, "I watched a National Rifle Association tournament." But when you break down the National Rifle Association into its initials (NRA), the *N* takes the vowel sound "en." Now with only the initials, you would correctly say, "I watched an NRA tournament."

Several consonants can have vowel sounds. A few that come to mind are: *f* sounds like "ef," *l* sounds like "el," *r* sounds like "are."

Be aware of words with a silent *h*. We say: an hour or an honor. According to *The American Heritage High School Dictionary*, the words *historic* and *historical* remain the only *h* sounded words that are correctly preceded by *an*:

> …an historic occasion
> …an historical event
> (See **historic** vs **historical**.)

When *u* takes the short vowel sound, use *an*. When the *u* takes the long vowel sound like "ewe" or "yew," use *a*.

> I took *an* umbrella.
> He was *a* unique sort of fellow—in *an* unusual way. (I don't know what this means, crittur, but it demonstrates my point.)

## Adjectives, Comparatively Speaking

You saw earlier (page 169) how some adverbs compare. Some adjectives also compare. As with adverbs, adjectives compare in comparative and superlative forms. Comparative adjectives compare two things, one to the other. Superlative adjectives compare three or more things.

| Adjective | Comparative | Superlative |
|-----------|-------------|-------------|
| cold | colder (of two) | coldest (of all) |
| nice | nicer (of two) | nicest (of all) |
| kind | kinder (of two) | kindest (of all) |

Remember the rules about comparing two things (one to the other) and three or more things. Comparisons can trip you up easy enough. Use your common sense, crittur, when you carry the comparison throughout your sentence.

> Incorrect: Of the two barrels of whiskey, this one is best.
>
> Correct: Of the two barrels of whiskey, this one is better.
>
> Correct: Of the three barrels of whiskey, this one is best.

> Incorrect: He is tougher than any man in the mountains. (Since he, too, is in the mountains, is he tougher than himself?)
>
> Correct: He is tougher than any other man in the mountains.
>
> Correct: He is the toughest of all the mountain men.

> Incorrect: Big Jake is the strongest of the two men.
>
> Correct: Big Jake is the stronger of the two men.
>
> Correct: Big Jake is the strongest smelling of all the men in camp.

*Good and Bad Adjectives*
Some adjectives take irregular form and become a different word in the comparative and superlative.

| Adjective | Comparative | Superlative |
|-----------|-------------|-------------|
| good | better | best |
| bad | worse | worst |
| many | more | most |

Most short adjectives become comparative by adding *er* and become superlative by adding *est*. Some adjectives, even short adjectives, are sometimes made comparative or superlative by putting the words *more* or *most* before it. Consult a dictionary when in doubt as to the correct comparative or superlative form.

When making a comparative or superlative with most adjectives ending in *y*, change the *y* to *i* and add *er* or *est*.

| Adjective | Comparative | Superlative |
|-----------|-------------|-------------|
| cagey | cagier | cagiest |
| spicy | spicier | spiciest |
| handy | handier | handiest |

For longer adjectives (usually three or more syllables), use *more* or *less* for the comparative and *most* or *least* for the superlative.

| Adjective | Comparative | Superlative |
|-----------|-------------|-------------|
| delicious | more delicious | most delicious |
| | less delicious | least delicious |
| formidable | more formidable | most formidable |
| | less formidable | least formidable |
| disconsolate | more disconsolate | most disconsolate |
| | less disconsolate | least disconsolate |

Never use *more* or *less* with a comparative adjective ending in *er*, or *most* or *least* with a superlative adjective ending in *est*.

When in doubt, even with shorter adjectives, you may be safe in using *more* or *less*, or *most* or *least*. At least it will sound good enough so you can pull it off in mixed company west of the Yellowstone. Still, it is always best to consult a dictionary.

> Incorrect: He was more better with a rifle than Tom Smith was.
>
> Correct: He was better with a rifle than Tom Smith was.

> Incorrect: He was more handier with a knife than Tom Smith was.
>
> West of the Yellowstone: He was more handy with a knife than Tom Smith was. (…than was Tom Smith.)
>
> Correct: He was handier with a knife than Tom Smith was. (…than was Tom Smith.)

> Incorrect: He was the most handiest of all.
>
> Incorrect: He was the least handiest of all.
>
> West of the Yellowstone: He was the most handy of all.
>
> Correct: He was the handiest of all.
>
> Correct: He was the least handy of all.

> Incorrect: It was the most spiciest of all the dishes.

Incorrect: It was more spicier.

West of the Yellowstone: It was more spicy.

Correct: It was spicier.

Correct: It was the spiciest of all the dishes.

### *Good* and *Well*

*Good* is always an adjective; it never modifies a verb. *Well* can be an adverb or an adjective depending on how it's used. When *well* relates to health, it is always an adjective. *Well* can be an adjective when it refers to appearance.

> He is a good swimmer. (The adjective *good* describes the noun *swimmer*.)
>
> He swims well. (The adverb *well* modifies the verb *swims*.)
>
> He seemed well. (*Well* is the predicate adjective following the linking verb *seemed*. We are really saying, "He *seemed* healthy.")
>
> His hat looked well on his head. (*Well* is the predicate adjective following the linking verb *looked*. We are really saying, the hat *appeared* appropriate or proper on his head.)

As an adjective, *well* can mean satisfactory, proper, fitting.

> All is well.
>
> It was well we decided to leave when we did.

He knew it was well to heed the chief's advice.

Finally, *well* can be an interjection.

Well, I'll be hog-tied and traded fer a mule!

---

## MUTANT MODIFIERS

(Also referred to as dangling participles, dangling phrases, dangling clauses.)

Warning: Even well-bred, well-intentioned modifiers can mutate into monsters. So, be ever on your guard. Always place an adjective phrase close to the noun or pronoun it describes, and always place an adverb or adverb phrase close to the word or words it modifies. To do otherwise is to court disaster. Behold the following Mutant Modifiers.

**Silly**: Many hunters shoot buffalo on horseback. (Are the buffalo on horseback, or are the hunters on horseback?)

**Better**: Many hunters on horseback shoot buffalo.

**Comical**: Having bandy legs, droopy ears, and little rat eyes, Big Jake was able to make a good trade for the old horse.

**Laughable**: Locoweed Louie came out of his tent on a cold morning and built a fire in his underwear.

You get the idea, crittur. This next one requires a little preface:

———◆►✕◄◆———

Aging meat tenderizes it and changes its enzymes to make it more flavorful. Aging is especially beneficial in preparing the meat of wild game animals. Not many Indians or mountain men bothered to age the meat of the game animals they harvested. Still, some did. The process was simple enough. A hunter would remove the entrails of a deer or elk (called "gutting" the animal). He would then spread open the carcass on a stick or two and hang it in a tree. Depending upon how cool the weather was—and the cool autumn was ideal—the hunter might leave the carcass hanging, drying, and turning rancid for several days. But only the outer meat would turn rancid. After several days, the hunter would cut away the rancid meat and leave it for the buzzards. At that point, the remaining inner meat was aged as well as one could expect under such primitive field conditions.

———◆►✕◄◆———

Now what does aging meat have to do with mutant modifiers? Suppose a writer, unmindful of mutant modifiers, had begun to write about aging meat in the following manner:

> When hung in a tree until rancid, you can enjoy perfectly aged venison.

> Aged and rotten, Big Jake enjoyed his buffalo meat by the open fire.

Here are some more mutant modifiers, crittur— just to kind of, sort of show you how not to write:

> Shot in the butt, Big Jake could only imagine how angry the wounded bear must be.
>
> Crawling through piles of horse plops, Big Jake found what looked like some interesting dung beetles.
>
> The trainer taught the dog owner to stop crotch sniffing.
>
> Big Jake discussed the chances of survival of a mountain man with three wives.
>
> Big Jake kept a portrait of his mother-in-law nailed to a tree over the campfire.

A mountain man knows life is like any other sporting event, and sometimes a crittur has to pick himself up and reach down and hitch things up and get himself set for the next play.

Here is how to correct sloppy writing and mutant modifiers that are not so readily recognized, even by the careful writer:

> Mutant: *A man known to husband his words,* not a complaint was ever heard from Big Jake about Iron Skillet's temper.

Correct: *A man known to husband his words*, Big Jake was never heard to complain about Iron Skillet's temper.

Mutant: *Savvy and ever watchful*, keeping Big Jake in line was no problem for Iron Skillet.

Correct: *Savvy and ever watchful*, Iron Skillet had no problem keeping Big Jake in line.

We need another preface here before we continue with our mutant modifiers:

In the dark of night, Iron Skillet lay asleep with Big Jake's arm beneath her head and shoulder. From somewhere deep in the wilderness, a coyote howled out its woes...

Mutant: As Iron Skillet snored and snorted and belched in her sleep, *the sheer folly of gnawing off his own arm, slipping out of the teepee, and making a wild, desperate run for it* crossed Big Jake's mind.

Correct: As Iron Skillet snored and snorted and belched in her sleep, Big Jake considered the sheer folly of gnawing off his own arm, slipping out of the teepee, and making a wild, desperate run for it.

Mutant: Reputed to be the most savage, few trappers were willing to cross Blackfeet Indian territory. (This is incorrect because it is not the trappers, but the *Blackfeet Indians* who were reputed to be the most savage.)

Correct: Reputed to be the most savage, the Blackfeet Indians found few trappers willing to cross their territory. (Keep the participle phrase and Blackfeet Indians close together.)

Good writing means good word choices and good sentence structure. Keep proofreading what you write. And keep rewriting.

Good going, crittur. You've come a long way. I hereby confer upon you the title of:

## ✹ MINISTER OF MODIFIERS ✹

# THE TAMED COUGAR AND THE DOMESTICATED MOUNTAIN MAN:

## Encountering the Elusive Verbal

*"His heart says more about a man than his tongue could ever say. So don't try to read anything in a man's eyes or even in his words. What a man does and how he does it says all you need to know about him."*

—SILAS POTTER

**B**ig Jake could call his dog or his horse without words or sounds. And he had only to think of Calls Down the Stars or to feel a vague longing for her, and she was at his side. He could trek the high country through the day and into the night, with the scents of the earth and the fallen leaves carried on the wind, his head swooning with the great mysteries of the deep valleys and endless forests, the great unknowable god of creation, the serene, primordial solitude filling his heart to bursting. He could watch the cold rain and mist blow over the mountain peaks and down across the valleys below. He could build a shelter, start a fire, sharpen his knife, clean his rifle, love a woman from the depths of his lonely heart, and never speak a word.

And in the frosty night, when Big Jake lay warm in the blankets with Calls Down the Stars, beneath the moon, beneath the dark treetops, the moan of the wind through the forest, it seemed he was in a far forever where all the brutal things he knew no longer threatened. And there was never a need for words.

———◆◆✖◆◆———

People who didn't know him may have labeled Big Jake a fool, but Big Jake was simply what he was—a mountain man, plain and true.

A verbal is like a tamed cougar or a domesticated mountain man. You never quite understand him, and you never completely trust him. As with Big Jake, many folks don't see verbals for what they are.

A verbal is a word formed from a verb but serving as another part of speech. Verbals can be *gerunds*, *infinitives*, or *participles*. The use of verbals makes for interesting sentence architecture. As we discuss verbals, take note of how gerunds, infinitives, and participles can vary sentence structure and enhance writing style.

## GERUNDS

A gerund is a strange entity. It is formed from a verb, so it can have a direct object. It can be modified by an adverb. But it serves as a noun, so it can be described by an adjective and by an adjective phrase. What is this strange creature?

A gerund is a present tense verb with *ing* as a suffix. A gerund is a word that was a verb until *ing* attached itself to its backside. You can do it yourself, crittur. Go on, be fearless—stalk a lone verb. Don't hurt it; just add *ing* to it, and then use it as a noun. Do it while no one's looking. After you build up your confidence, you'll want to do it publicly and shamelessly.

Once you add the *ing*, the verb becomes a verbal, masquerading as, and assuming almost all the functions of, a noun: subject of a sentence, direct object, object of the preposition, or predicate noun. Maybe, if I work on it long enough, I can get a gerund to serve as an indirect object. Gentle readers and all knowing critturs are invited to weigh in on this one.

The following sentences serve as examples of how gerunds are used:

> Among other things, singing requires lyrics about cheatin', boozin', and brawlin', a drunken mountain man with great lung capacity, and the ability to hit the proper notes. Two out of three ain't bad. (*Sing*

is a verb, but add *ing*, and *sing* becomes *singing*. *Singing*, as a noun, serves as the subject of the sentence. *Requires* is the verb.)

Hunting is great sport. (*Hunt* is a verb until you add *ing* to it. *Hunting* is the subject of this sentence.)

In late autumn and early spring, mountain men went trapping for prime furs. (*Trap* can be a noun or verb, but *trapping* is a gerund. As a noun, *trapping* is the direct object of the verb *went*.)

To the old chief, Shadow in the Thicket, lying was equivalent to stealing. (*Lie* is a verb, but *lying* is a noun and the subject of the sentence. *Steal* is a verb, but *stealing* is a noun and the object of the preposition *to*.)

## Gerund Phrase

A gerund phrase is a phrase consisting of a gerund, its object, and its modifier.

(See Phrases and Clauses.)

Amassing a store of plews was the goal of the trappers. (*Amassing* is a gerund; *store* is its object.)

Consistently surviving Indians, wild predators, and the elements was a challenge. (*Surviving* is a gerund; *consistently* is an adverb modifying *surviving*.)

> Wilderness skills, quick wits, and accurate shooting ensured a mountain man's survival. (*Shooting* is a gerund; *accurate* is an adjective describing *shooting*.)

Remember the tamed cougar and the domesticated mountain man we spoke of earlier? You never quite understand them, and you never completely trust them. Well, put gerunds into that category. A gerund slips easily in and out of character. A gerund is a gerund except when it is preceded by a helping (auxiliary) verb. Once a gerund is preceded by a helping verb, the gerund reverts to being a verb.

> Gerund: (*running*) Big Jake knew *running* was good for his health.
>
> **or**
>
> Big Jake knew; *running* was good for his health.

> Verb: (*was running*) Big Jake *was running* for his life from the Utes.

## Gerund or Participle?

All right, crittur, this is a test:

To form a gerund you add *ing* to a present tense verb. To form a present participle you add *ing* to a present tense verb. So, how do you tell the difference between a gerund and a participle?

No, no, crittur, don't guess. And don't go back and check. That's cheating. You either know, or you don't know. Okay, time's up. Follow closely. Ask yourself:

How is the word used in a sentence? When the *ing*-verbal is used as a noun, it is a gerund. When it is used as a modifier, it is a participle.

> Trading fairly with the Indians allowed a man to keep his scalp. (*Trading fairly* is a gerund phrase, the subject of the sentence, and the subject of the verb *allowed*.)
>
> Trading fairly with the Indians, a man was sure to keep his scalp. (Used here, *trading fairly* is a participle phrase describing or modifying the noun *man*. *Man* is the subject of the sentence.)

So now you know, crittur. Isn't this exciting stuff? With enough practice, you'll be ready for infinitives.

———◆◆◆◆———

Big Jake had an easy smile and a flash of white teeth that always warmed the heart of Calls Down the Stars. His smile could brighten her mornings or calm her fears in the dark of night. She learned to return his smile, which was not something an Indian woman did as easily as a white woman. She would smile to herself as she lay warm against him in the night, her long hair across his shoulder, her eyes closed in the darkness, listening to his steady breathing as his big chest rose and fell.

———◆◆◆◆———

# INFINITIVES

An infinitive is a basic verb form preceded by the word *to*. *To hunt, to trap, to swim, to ride, to shoot, to trade* are all infinitives. Now I'm not sure why they call them infinitives, except maybe that you can stick all manner of extraneous words inside an infinitive and in that way the infinitive can go on for, well, infinity. We'll discuss that in the section on split infinitives. For now, just know that you can use infinitives and infinitive phrases as nouns, adjectives, and adverbs.

## *Infinitives as Subject Nouns*

Infinitives and infinitive phrases can be used any way a noun can be used. As a noun, an infinitive can serve as the subject of a sentence.

> To err is human, to forgive divine. (*To err* is the subject of the sentence. The comma makes the second infinitive elliptical.) (See Commas.)
>
> "To die would be a blessing," Big Jake whispered as he woke up with a hangover after a three-day binge. (*To die* is the subject of Big Jake's sentence.)
>
> To trade with the Rees was suicidal. (The subject of this sentence is the infinitive phrase *to trade with the Rees*.)

## *Infinitives as Object Nouns*

As a noun, an infinitive can also be the object of a sentence.

I wish *to sleep*. (*To sleep* is the infinitive.
Here the infinitive serves as the object of
the verb *wish*.)

All good mountain men learn *to trap*. (*To
trap* is the direct object of the verb
*learn*.)

The trapper learns *to live a stark existence*.
(The infinitive phrase *to live a stark
existence* is the object of the verb
*learns*.)

## Infinitives as Adjectives

When an infinitive or an infinitive phrase describes a
noun or pronoun, it serves as an adjective.

A string of packhorses loaded with pelts
was a sight *to see*. (The infinitive *to see*
serves as an adjective describing or
modifying the predicate noun *sight*.)

Mountain man Jim Bridger was a man *to
respect*. (The infinitive *to respect* is an
adjective describing *man*.)

## Infinitives as Adverbs

When an infinitive or an infinitive phrase modifies a
verb, an adjective, or an adverb, it serves as an
adverb.

The Indians came *to meet Jim Bridger*.
(The infinitive phrase *to meet Jim
Bridger* serves as an adverb modifying
the verb *came*.)

The regal bull elk was magnificent *to behold*. (The infinitive *to behold* is now an adverb modifying the predicate adjective *magnificent*.)

Infinitives, all of which begin with *to*, should not be confused with the preposition *to*. The word *to* is a preposition when it is followed by a noun or pronoun (the object of the preposition). *To* is a "sign of the infinitive" when it is followed by a verb.

Let's go *to* the mountains *to* live. (The first *to* is a preposition and begins the prepositional phrase *to the mountains*. The second *to* is a sign of the infinitive. *To live* is the infinitive.)

Sometimes the infinitive is understood. In the following sentence, you are really saying, "Shoot if you have *to shoot*." The infinitive *to shoot* is understood.

Shoot if you have *to*.

An infinitive is usually preceded by the word *to*—but not always. When an infinitive follows certain verbs or their variations (*let, hear, help, make*, etc.), the *to* is sometimes omitted.

When you say:

The Indians help the trappers locate beaver colonies.

You are really saying:

> The Indians help the trappers *to locate* beaver colonies.

When you say:

> The Indians let the mountain men cross their land.

You are really saying:

> The Indians permitted the mountain men *to cross* their land.

Infinitives are a verb form, and like verbs they can have objects and be modified by adverbs. An infinitive, its object, and modifiers constitute an infinitive phrase.

> Back then it seemed impossible *to conquer* the vast wilderness. (*Wilderness* is the direct object of *to conquer*.)
>
> The forbidding mountains promised *to offer* adventurers untold fortunes. (*Fortunes* is the direct object and *adventurers* is the indirect object of *to offer*.)
>
> In spite of hardships and hostile Indians, adventurers, fortune hunters, and simple trappers continued *to tramp* westward. (*Westward* is the adverb modifying *to tramp*.)

## Split Infinitives

A split infinitive is the dreaded occurrence of modifiers placed between the word *to* and the verb in the infinitive. It is called splitting the infinitive, and it's especially egregious when a writer sticks half a dozen adverbs between the *to* and the verb.

It is true that splitting an infinitive sometimes sounds awkward and should be avoided. But a split infinitive is not always as sinister as grammarians would have you believe. In the third example below, the split is just fine as it stands.

> Awkward: In the wild beauty of the mountains, the trapper loved *to* peacefully *wander*.
>
> Better: In the wild beauty of the mountains, the trapper loved *to wander* peacefully.
>
> Just fine: When the fur trade finally died, the mountain men had *to* carefully *reassess* their prospects.

How does a writer know if a split infinitive is all right? Well, when it's wrong, the main idea of what is being stated seems to rest on the wrong word. Try it yourself, and you'll readily see when a split infinitive is just wrong for the sentence. Somehow, the first sentence below strains the brain as the reader tries to follow along. The second sentence flows, and the meaning and message of the sentence seems almost effortless—as all sentences should be.

> Strains the brain: The trapper loved to peacefully wander.
>
> Flows effortlessly: The trapper loved to wander peacefully.

---

## PARTICIPLES

Varying your sentences with participles and participle phrases adds style and verve to your writing. But keep your brain engaged for this one, crittur, and follow assiduously. Participles are sly.

Add the suffix *ing* to verbs to form present participles. Add the suffix *ed* to most regular verbs to form past participles. A participle can serve as a verb and take an object, or serve as an adjective to describe a noun or pronoun. Here's where participles are sly: If the *ing* word serves as a noun, it is gerund, not a participle.

All right, let's get into this. In the following sentence, *playing* is a participle describing *Big Jake*. *Coming* is a gerund because it is the object of the preposition *before*. *Was stuffing* is the verb.

> Playing gleefully, before coming to his senses, Big Jake was stuffing beans up Iron Skillet's nose while she slept.
>
> Participle as verb and adjective: The trapper *setting* his traps is Big Jake. (*Setting* is a verb because it has an object, *traps*. It is an adjective because it describes or modifies the noun *trapper*. The predicate is the linking verb *is*.)

Participle as adjective: A *tanned* elk hide commands a lot of money in St. Louis. (*Tanned* is an adjective describing or modifying the noun *hide*—or *elk hide* if you consider it one entity.)

Participle as predicate adjective: The old timer's disdain of modern man was all *encompassing*. (*Encompassing* is the predicate adjective describing the subject noun *disdain*.)

As shown above, participles can serve as verbs. Add auxiliary verbs into the mix and participles become verb phrases.

am playing, have played, are paddling, had paddled

To vary your writing, learn to master verbals. Use present and past participles as adjectives, describing nouns or pronouns.

*Bristling*, Big Jake endured the preacher's scathing condemnation. (Here *bristling* is an adjective describing the noun *Big Jake*.)

*Confused*, he finally lashed out at the preacher. (Here *confused* is an adjective describing the pronoun *he*.)

The *berated* mountain man balled up his fists and planted his feet. (*Berated* is an adjective describing the noun *mountain man*.)

The thought of Iron Skillet *screaming* and *cursing* sent shivers down his spine. (The participles *screaming* and *cursing* serve as adjectives. The subject of the sentence is *thought*. The predicate is *sent*. The reason why *screaming* and *cursing* are participles and not gerunds is because they serve as adjectives describing Iron Skillet. Besides, in this sentence context, you would use a possessive noun or possessive pronoun before a gerund—if we had gerunds, not participles. Are you following this, crittur?)

Participles are born of verbs and as such can take objects and be modified by adverbs. When you combine a participle, its object, and its modifier, you have a participle phrase.

*Exceptionally irritated*, Big Jake breathed an oath of enviable profanity. (*Exceptionally irritated* is a participle phase describing the noun *Big Jake*. *Exceptionally* is an adverb modifying the participle *irritated* which serves as an adjective. See how easy this is?)

*Clenching his teeth*, Big Jake took a round house punch at the preacher, hitting him squarely in the chops. (*Clenching his teeth* is a participle phrase describing the noun *Big Jake*. *Teeth* is the object of the participle *clenching*.)

*Crossing the divide,* Jedediah Smith descended into the valley. (*Crossing the divide* is a participle phrase describing the noun *Jedediah Smith. Divide* is the object of the participle *crossing.*)

One more thing, crittur. A participle is no longer a participle when it is combined with a helping (auxiliary) verb. With the helping verb, the *ing* word remains a verb.

> *Walking* all day, he grew tired. (Here *walking* is a participle.)
>
> He *had been walking* all day and was tired. (Here *walking*—more precisely, *had been walking*—is a verb or verb phrase.)

## The Dreaded "Dangling Participle"

A word, or two or three, of caution regarding participle phrases. Keep your participle phrase close to the word or words it modifies. Make sure a participle phrase connects logically with the subject of the sentence, otherwise you have a dangling participle or some other mutant modifier with which to contend. When a conjunction, an appositive, an adjective, or an adjective phrase comes before a participle phrase, this caution still applies.

> Mutant: *After being adopted by the chief,* the Indians greeted Big Jake as one of their own.

> Correct: *After being adopted by the chief,*
> Big Jake was greeted by the Indians as
> one of their own.
>
> Correct: *Immediately after being adopted*
> *by the chief,* Big Jake was greeted by the
> Indians as one of their own.

A dangling participle is one of several mutant modifiers that can make even a practiced writer look pretty silly. Be careful, crittur; mutant modifiers take on sinister forms and cause embarrassments even your best friends will find amusing. You may gain or lose a reputation on the silly stuff.

> Sitting at the table with a knife and fork,
> careful to balance his napkin properly
> on his lap, the goat soon made a tasty
> meal.
>
> Singing "Buffalo Gals" and playing his har-
> monica, the snake surprised Locoweed
> Louie on the trail.
>
> *Standing in his underwear,* Locoweed
> Louie saw Big Jake getting smacked in
> the head by Iron Skillet wielding her fry
> pan. (This sentence is correct if it is
> Locoweed Louie standing in his under-
> wear. If Big Jake is standing in his
> underwear, you need to recast the sen-
> tence.)
>
> Locoweed Louie saw Big Jake standing
> there getting smacked in the head by
> Iron Skillet in his underwear. (Well,

that's not right either, unless Iron Skillet is wearing Big Jake's or Locoweed Louie's underwear. Let's try it again.)

Locoweed Louie saw Big Jake standing in his underwear getting smacked in the head by Iron Skillet. (Now we get the picture.)

Good job, crittur. You're getting it now. I hereby confer upon you the title of:

## ✶ Savior of the Verbals ✶

# My Stick Floats with Yours:

---

## Conjunctions and Transitions

T he old mountain man understood women considerably less than he understood the wild creatures he hunted and trapped. Most mountain men—not all, of course—could no more be cruel to a woman than be cruel to an animal in the forest. When he loved a woman who proved unmanageable, many a mountain man rode off or simply walked into the sunset, and was gone. Some women appreciated that freedom of spirit. Finding their men gone, other women were bitterly resentful of the unvented fury they were denied.

For as dumb as some folks thought he was, Stinky Petey knew about conjunctions and transitions. He knew to be conjoined to a woman in marriage would mean some major transitions in his life he was unwilling to abide: bathing regularly, keeping his clothes relatively clean, keeping a woman fed, and staying out of saloons and jails.

Stinky Petey pursued some gals whenever the mood struck him and whenever a gal was available, but when it got to where the gal started getting that look of intent in her eye, Stinky Petey was gone. He didn't hold with the foofaraw; he thought a gal high-toned if she wore clean socks every day. And for as dumb as others thought he was, Stinky Petey knew how to use words. If he could talk a gal out of her socks, he could talk her out of any thoughts of matrimony.

"Ya got money, do you, eh?" was a question Stinky Petey had found to work reasonably well on any gal who tarried with whatever amorous look he considered threatening. There were other questions and off-handed comments equally efficacious:

"Ya got any whiskey, lady?" and "If-in' ya got a husband, how soon ya 'spectin' him back?"

And as he left a gal, Stinky Petey could be heard to lament, "If-in' I left anything in that jug o' whiskey, lady, I shore is sorry."

There exists no record of any marriage between Stinky Petey and any woman west of the Mississippi. And it's doubtful any woman ever pursued Stinky Petey except maybe to find him and kill him.

## CONJUNCTIONS

A conjunction is a word that joins other words or groups of words in a sentence. Some common conjunctions are: *and, or, but, however, then, before,* etc. As a general rule, if you need a comma with a conjunction, the comma goes before the conjunction. You usually need a comma before a conjunction when a conjunction joins two independent clauses. Avoid putting a comma after a conjunction, but, sadly, sometimes you must.

You don't always need a comma with a conjunction. Usually, if a conjunction is not joining two independent clauses, no comma is needed. In the first sentence below, a conjunction joins a compound subject. In the second sentence, a conjunction joins a compound verb. The conjunction in the third sentence joins a compound object. The last two are compound sentences, the only sentences where a comma and conjunction are needed because independent clauses are joined together.

> Wiley Willie and Sagebrush Sam sat at the campfire.
> They smoked their pipes and listened to the wolves howl in the hills.
> The fire spit out smoke and sparks.
> He was good rider, and Jake was a good shot.
> She was Nelly O'Grady, and she was as tough as any man.

Use a semicolon to separate the independent clauses of a compound sentence when you do not use a conjunction.

(See Commas and Semicolons.)

> He was plenty tough; he was a mountain man.

If the second element of the sentence is not an independent clause, only the conjunction is needed. In the following sentence, however, you may opt to place a comma before the conjunction, just for clarity and emphasis.

> She was tough, but exceedingly pretty.

Transition words can be effective conjunctions. Transition words tip off the reader to a change in thought or focus. A transition word usually precedes an important second element in a sentence.

> He hired on as the camp cook, though he was the deadliest shot in the company.

Use commas between words in a series when only one conjunction is used. Place the last comma before the conjunction. Do not use a comma after the last word in the series. Do not use commas between words in a series if all the words in a series are separated by *and* or *or*.

> The buffalo raged, bellowed, snorted, and stomped before it thundered across the prairie at the men and horses trying to get out of its path.
> The river was wide and fast and dangerously cold.

## *But*

*But* is a perfectly respectable conjunction, as fine as they come. But *but* is redundant following *doubt* and *help*.

> Redundant: Zeke Hatcher had no doubt but that Parker Daniels deserved to hang.
> Correct: Zeke Hatcher had no doubt that Parker Daniels deserved to hang.

> Redundant: Parker Daniels could not help but hear the shouts of the gathering mob.
> Correct: Parker Daniels could not help hearing the shouts of the gathering mob.

Remember, too, *but* is not always a conjunction. It is at times a preposition or an adverb. When it is not a conjunction, *but* requires no comma. When *but* is a conjunction joining a compound sentence and followed by a pronoun, the pronoun should be a subject pronoun. When *but* is a preposition, followed by a pronoun, the pronoun should be an object pronoun.

> Iron Skillet couldn't cook worth a summer plew, but she sure could eat.
> Not a crittur liked her stew but her.

That's simple enough, most of the time, to a crittur who avoids elliptical construction. But things have a way of getting confusing when part of the sentence is supposed to be understood. It's like saying: "I paint people in the nude." Who's nude, you or the people you are painting? See what I mean?

If the first sentence below were written out, a comma properly placed before the conjunction *but* would make the meaning clear, and the correct use of the subject pronoun would be evident. In the second sentence, *but* is a preposition, not a conjunction, and an object pronoun needs to follow as the object of the preposition. Both sentences below are said to be correct.

> All the trappers were weary but he (was not weary).
> All the trappers were weary but him.

Stick with me on this one, crittur; you may be the only friend I have. Placing your *but* closer to the beginning or the middle of the sentence does not solve the problem. In the following sentence, *but* is still a preposition; however, as used here, many grammarians consider the subject pronoun acceptable. I do not, crittur.

> All the trappers but he were weary.

I, personally, would end all controversy by simply finding a better, clearer way to write the sentence. And I would swear off ellipses forever.

In the following sentences, *but* is a preposition meaning *with the exception of* or *except for*. No comma is needed here. Because *but* is a preposition, you would need the objective case pronoun *him* to replace *Stinky Petey*.

> No one came to the party but Stinky Petey.
> No one came to the party but him.

Finally, *but* can be an adverb meaning *only* or *just*. No comma is needed in the next sentence.

> He had but one bullet left.

## Conjunctive Adverbs

A conjunctive adverb does just what its name indicates. It's an adverb that joins or connects two thoughts. Some conjunctive adverbs are: *besides, furthermore, moreover, however, nevertheless, nonetheless, so, still, then, yet, otherwise, consequently, as a result, thus.* Place a semicolon before, and a comma after a conjunctive adverb when the conjunctive adverb joins two independent clauses (two complete sentences in a compound sentence).

> Incorrect: She was a shrew of a woman, thus, Big Jake was wont to avoid whiskey, women, gambling, chewin', spitting, cussin', fightin', belchin', and speaking up when he was in her presence.
> Correct: She was a shrew of a woman; thus, Big Jake was wont to avoid whiskey, women, gambling, chewin', spitting, cussin', fightin', belchin', and speaking up when he was in her presence.

> Incorrect: To take their pelts out of the mountains, most trappers used pack-horses, however, some favored canoes.
>
> Correct: To take their pelts out of the mountains, most trappers used packhorses; however, some favored canoes.

> Correct: Running from stampeding buffalo can actually be good for the cardiovascular system; nonetheless, I'd rather be on a hillside watching some other hapless petitioner-to-heaven get his exercise.

Rendezvous was an annual gathering, a celebration of camaraderie and ribald decadence. It brought together mountain men and company agents, trappers and supply wagons, scouts, Indians, Indian squaws, tobacco, whiskey, games, riotous singing and dancing, and things better left to the imagination.

Rendezvous separated men from their senses, their money, and sometimes from a season's worth of plews, their best horse, and their best wife. In the following examples, you will notice that a conjunctive adverb is not always the first word following the semicolon.

> Rendezvous was a summer event; nonetheless, Big Jake would attempt to stretch it into autumn.
>
> Rendezvous was a summer event; Big Jake, nonetheless, would attempt to stretch it into autumn.

> Rendezvous was a summer event; Big Jake would, nonetheless, attempt to stretch it into autumn.
>
> Rendezvous was a summer event; Big Jake would attempt, nonetheless, to stretch it into autumn.
>
> Rendezvous was a summer event; Big Jake would attempt to stretch it into autumn, nonetheless.

## *Using* **However**

Use the semicolon before, and the comma after *however* when it states a conditional or contrasting relationship between the elements of a sentence. However, when *however* is strictly a conjunction intended to mean "regardless of how," no semicolon or comma is needed.

> When a warrior staked himself out in battle, he was there to fight to the death however savage his end might be.

## **And, But, Or**

Remember, *and,* *but,* and *or* are conjunctions, not conjunctive adverbs.

## *Using* **Than**

*Than* is a much misused word. Although its meanings are few, they are varied, indeed. *Than* can be a conjunction or a preposition. But a word or two here about *than* as a preposition. If you ever use *than* as a preposition, crittur, please don't ever tell anyone you knew me.

As a preposition, the word *than* has some weird old stuffy applications no self-respecting mountain man would ever use—not if he ever wanted to look at himself in the mirror again. Could you imagine a mountain man saying: "He was an Indian scout than whom I can fancy no hoss more competent." Why, critturs would laugh that dude off three mountains, clear across the Yellowstone, and down across the wide prairies on back to St. Louis and parts east. He'd be lucky they didn't string him up to the nearest tree, except maybe they'd want to keep him alive for the sheer entertainment of his company.

Fortunately, we will consider only the conjunction *than*. Most dictionaries will tell you *than* is a conjunction used to usher a gentleman and squire a lady gently into the second element of an unequal comparison.

That horse was smarter than my dog.

But that's just the beginning. A crittur needs to be specific when using *than* to compare. If a following verb is suggested or understood, the writer should write out the verb. Otherwise, he creates unnecessary confusion.

I am trusted more by the Cheyenne than the Blackfeet.

Are you really saying:

I am trusted more by the Cheyenne than the Blackfeet (are trusted by them).

Or, are you saying:

> I am trusted more by the Cheyenne *than I am trusted* by the Blackfeet.

When pronouns follow *than*, be just as vigilant. And here, too, as in the previous example where trust was in question between or among the Cheyenne and Blackfeet, it is best to flesh out your sentence with the missing words.

Some grammarians will tell you the following sentences are correct because of their assumed elliptical meaning. But remember, when the sentence ends with an object pronoun (*me*), *than* is being used as a preposition followed by its object. The other sentence ends with the subject pronoun *I* and means something entirely different.

> Big Jake is braver than I.
> But the dawn attack scared him more than me.

The first sentence is said to be correct because it is assumed to be elliptical for: Big Jake is braver than I am. The second sentence is said to be equally correct because it is assumed to be elliptical for: But the dawn attack scared him more than it scared me.

This is a good place, crittur, for a little extra learning—and it won't cost you any extra. Here it is: The same rules as *than* apply when *as* is used in comparison.

> You won't find as smart a coon as I. (…as I
>     am.)

Bow-tied grammarians and soft-shod city folk will caution that in formal writing one should never use the elliptical. I am loath to throw in with such specimens, but I must admit, they tell it well.

All right, I'll admit, we all use elliptical sentences at times. Even me. I mean, even I. Let's end it this way: On its own, when a sentence is not elliptical, avoid using *than* as a preposition followed by an object pronoun. The following sentence is never correct.

> Big Jake is braver than me.

You're advancing quickly, crittur. Look how far you've come. I hereby confer upon you the title of:

### ❋ CONQUEROR OF THE CONJUNCTION ❋

# CLAWS OF THE CLAUSE, FORAYS OF THE PHRASE:

---

## Subduing Clauses and Phrases

---

*"Sometimes it's best to love a woman from a distance."*

⟨SILAS POTTER⟩

There were nasty claw marks that left old scars along Big Jake's face and down his chest. Sometimes men kidded him about the scars being the triumphs and losses in his marriage to Iron Skillet, but they knew. Some time in the long ago, Big Jake had a one-on-one bout with an angry grizzly and the big man had come out the winner. Well, you can call him a winner because he survived and the bruin didn't, but Big Jake had lost some flesh and bone, and a lot of blood in the encounter. If Big Jake had gained a reputation for being more than just a fool, it didn't stop him from bragging up the fool.

"I'm fleet as a buff'lo runner," he'd bellow, "stronger than a bull, tougher than a b'ar, dumber than dog in the sun chasin' his shadow. Other critturs—they have their dark side. I don't have no dark side. I have a backside. A big one! I'm an ass! Any man want to make somethin' of that can take a number and stand in line. Me? I'm gonna go find a cold beer somewhere—an' a plug o' chaw—an' a fine woman who's blind—blind and stupid 'nuff t' have me! Now let an ass through an' get out my way—an' start yer fightin' without me!"

Well, if the claws of a grizzly didn't phase Big Jake, clauses and phrases shouldn't scare off a child learning grammar. So, hone your Green River keen, crittur, and follow along. Keep abreast of me, and keep a wary eye. And be fearless.

Okay, here's an easy way for you to understand clauses and phrases: The independent clause is the boss of the outfit, standing alone and not countin' on anyone else to clarify what he says or make his point for him. The dependent clause is his little brother, a greenhorn, tagging along because he hasn't got the wherewithal to make it on his own. The phrase is the hired hand with no stake in anything, whose only job is to carry the extra gear and try to be useful. Now that should be all I need to tell you about clauses and phrases, but throw another log on the fire, crittur, and listen up.

# CLAUSES

## *Independent Clause*

An independent clause has a subject and verb and can stand alone as a complete sentence. A simple sentence is an independent clause; that is, it has a subject and a verb and expresses a complete thought.

The stars shone brightly overhead.

## *Subordinate Clause (or Dependent Clause)*

A subordinate clause may or may not have a subject and verb, but either way, it does not express a complete thought. Subordinate clauses usually begin with: *after, although, as, because, before, how, if, once, since, that, though, those, til, unless, until, what, whatever, when, whenever, where, wherever, which, who, whoever, whom, whomever, whose.*

A subordinate clause can serve as an adjective and be an adjective clause, serve as an adverb and be an adverb clause, or serve as a noun and be a noun clause.

> While the two men sat at the campfire... (Delete *while* and you have a complete sentence.)
> Unless I'm mistaken... (Delete *unless* and you have a complete sentence.)
> Until I saw it for myself... (Delete *until* and you have a complete sentence.)

If you join an independent clause with a subordinate clause, you must have a word (or words) that joins them, but you do not need a comma.

> Are you going to fight or run?
> Are you going to fight, or are you going to run?

You need a comma before a conjunction only when the conjunction joins two independent clauses (two sentences) together; otherwise, do not use the comma—except for clarity.

> They kissed and made up.
> They kissed, and they made up.
>
> I'd be in Santa Fe but for you.
> I'd be in Santa Fe, but you need me here.

Here's what I mean by using a comma for clarity. In the sentences below, the conjunction *and* does not join two sentences, but the comma is needed to keep the reader from going back over the sentence to make sure he read it right the first time.

> The grizzly caught the scent of wood smoke and bacon, and lumbered down to the edge of camp.
> She was tall and pretty, and tough as any man.

For short compound sentences, it is acceptable to omit the comma.

They raved and they cussed.
The wind blew and the trees swayed.
The snow fell but they kept warm.

*Adverb Clause*

An adverb clause is a subordinate clause that thinks it's an adverb. Adverb clauses usually begin with transition words (usually adverbs or conjunctions) such as: *as, after, because, before, even as, even though, if, since, unless, until, when, where.* If you omit the transition word beginning the clause, the clause can stand as a complete sentence. The sentences below, however, read much smoother when adverb clauses are used.

The mountain men trapped. The beaver became scarce.
The mountain men trapped *until the beaver became scarce.*

He wandered the mountains. The mountain man discovered the high peaks, the valleys, the streams, the passes, the grazing land, the badlands, the forests, and swamps.
*As he wandered the mountains*, the mountain man discovered the high peaks, the valleys, the streams, the passes, the grazing land, the badlands, the forests, and swamps.

The beaver were gone. The mountain man found employment guiding the wagon trains west.

*When the beaver were gone,* the mountain man found employment guiding the wagon trains west.

## PHRASES

A phrase is a grouping of related words that do not have a subject and verb. A phrase can serve as an adjective and be an adjective phrase, serve as an adverb and be an adverb phrase, or serve as a noun and be a noun phrase.

### *Adverb Phrase*

A prepositional phrase that modifies a verb, an adjective, or another adverb is an adverb phrase or adverb prepositional phrase. Remember, a phrase does not contain a subject and verb. And remember to keep the adverb phrase close to the word it modifies so you don't end up with a mutant modifier.

The Cheyenne wandered *in search of game.* (*In* is the preposition; *game* is the object of the preposition. The adverb phrase modifies the verb *wandered.*)

The knife blade was keen *as a razor.* (*As* is the preposition; *razor* is the object of the preposition. The adverb phrase modifies the adjective *keen.*)

He shot wide *of the mark.* (*Of* is the preposition; *mark* is the object of the preposition. The adverb phrase modifies the adverb *wide.*)

Mountain men load their season's take of plews *in canoes* or *on the back* of packhorses. (The two adverb phrases *in canoes* and *on the back* modify the verb *load. Of packhorses* is not an adverb phrase; it is an adjective phrase describing or modifying the noun *back.*)

## Adjective Phrases and Adjective Clauses

All right, crittur, I don't have to hold your hand through this. I've quit calling you "gentle reader," in case you haven't noticed. That's because you're almost a full-fledged coon now. So, it's out of respect, not orneriness that I group together adjective clauses and adjective phrases under the same heading. You can handle it, crittur.

For style and dramatic effect, you will want to vary your sentences with adjective phrases and adjective clauses. When a prepositional phrase describes or modifies a noun or a pronoun, it is called an adjective phrase or an *adjective prepositional phrase.* An adjective clause or adjective phrase usually follows immediately after the noun or pronoun it describes, otherwise you may have a mutant modifier on your hands.

Adjective phrases and clauses are usually preceded by a relative pronoun (*that, what, which, who, whoever, whom, whomever, whose*), but may begin with *when, where,* or *why.* A relative pronoun relates the adjective clause to its noun antecedent or pronoun antecedent in the main clause. The relative pronoun may sometimes be omitted.

> Jim Bridger is a mountain man whom I trust.
>
> Jim Bridger is a mountain man I trust.

> The Black Hills which the Indians considered sacred could be seen from across the wide, rolling plains.
>
> The Black Hills the Indian considered sacred could be seen from across the wide, rolling plains.

> In those hills were red pipestone quarries that the white man blasted through in his search for gold.
>
> In those hills were red pipestone quarries the white man blasted through in his search for gold.

Nonrestrictive adjective phrases or adjective clauses should be set off with commas. Restrictive phrases or clauses do not require commas.

> This is the valley *that has the sweetest grass for grazing.* (*That* is the subject of *has.* The clause is restrictive.)
>
> The grasslands, *which you describe,* are over the next mountain. (*Which* is the

object of *describe*. The clause is nonrestrictive.)

The river winds down to the valley *of which you spoke*. (*Which* is the object of the preposition *of*. The clause is restrictive.)

Big Jake is the one *who discovered the pass*. (*Who* is the subject of *discovered*. The clause is restrictive.)

The old scout told us about a mountain pass *with a grisly history*. (This prepositional phrase is a restrictive adjective phrase describing *pass*—or *mountain pass* if you consider *mountain pass* as one entity.)

The bones, *which lay buried*, would never be found. (nonrestrictive adjective phrase)

The brave *who counts the most coup* garners the highest honors. (restrictive adjective clause)

Big Jake is searching for the ponies *that the Indians borrowed*. (restrictive adjective clause)

He carried a knife *with a very sharp blade*. (*With* is the preposition, *blade* is the object of the preposition. The adjective phrase describes the noun *knife*.)

The warrior *with the crooked smile* took an uninspired shot *at the white man*. (The prepositional phrase *with the crooked smile* becomes an adjective phrase when it describes the noun *warrior*. The prepositional phrase *at the white man* is an adjective phrase describing the noun *shot*.)

An adjective phrase has no subject or verb and cannot stand on its own and make sense. Still, it is content to be an adjective, and happy knowing it varies the sentence quite nicely, thank you. Sometimes it is simple and subtle, but always it is effective. Use phrases and clauses wisely, crittur.

The Medicine Man told a tale *about spirits*.

We've crossed another mountain, crittur. You've stuck with me through some rough spots. I hereby confer upon you the title of:

## ✳ Defender of Clauses and ✳ Guardian of Phrases

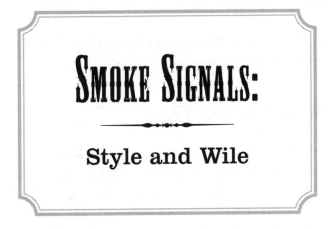

# SMOKE SIGNALS:

## Style and Wile

Anthropologists, archaeologists, paleontologists, and learned scholars were pretty unanimous in declaring the dog as man's first domesticated animal. In earlier years Big Jake might have sloshed down his rum, laughed out loud, and concurred. Then Big Jake met Iron Skillet. After Iron Skillet, all rum and laughter became a thing of the past. After Iron Skillet, Big Jake knew the dog was not man's first domesticated animal. Man's first domesticated animal was woman, with mixed results.

———◆◆◇◆◆———

Style is what is often called mechanics. It is not real writing style as Hemingway would have described it. Maybe think of the mechanics as the nuts-and-bolts components of style. Maybe someday soon I'll write a book called *The Mountain Man's*

*Field Guide to Writing and Storytelling.* Then I'll really get into writing style.

---

## NUMBERS AND TIME

### Writing Numbers as Figures or Words

Generally, you should spell numbers that begin a sentence, except when a year begins a sentence. But why would you begin a sentence with a year in numerals when it's easy enough to recast your sentence?

> Correct, but ugly: 1837–38 was a profitable
> fur season for Big Jake.
> Correct, and prettier: The 1837–38 fur sea-
> son was profitable for Big Jake.

In formal writing, formal invitations, announcements, and legal documents, spell out the year.

> …the seventeenth of May, one thousand
> eight hundred and forty-five.

Spell the numbers *zero* through *ten* and *first* through *tenth* anywhere in the sentence. Use numerals for all other numbers. Spell out large numbers. Hyphenate numbers ending in *y* when you join them to other word numbers (thirty-five, sixty-one, etc.).

> At camp that morning, 22 men showed up.
> (An iconoclastic crittur writing a cre-
> ative story or poem may spell out short

numbers such as twenty-two as long as there aren't additional bunches of numbers that would confuse the reader.)

Twenty-two men showed up at camp that morning.

There were a million reasons to turn back to camp. Big Jake would hear none of them.

You may write numerals for numbers in a series, but in formal writing or creative writing, spell out round numbers. You may opt to omit the word *and* between thousands, hundreds, tens, etc. as shown in the last two examples below.

That week the trappers caught 13 beavers and 6 hares. Two snarling wolves had to be shot.

They scouted along thirty miles of the valley.

They traveled two hundred and fifty miles.

They traveled two hundred fifty miles.

If numbers in a sentence refer to unrelated items—especially if the numbers are next to each other—differentiate the numbers by spelling out one number and not the other.

In 1821, fourteen trappers left St. Louis for the Rockies.

The following examples are correct for writing dates and time, depending on a writer's preference. In denoting a decade, the *s* alone is probably more widely accepted; the author, however (who is slightly more seasoned), prefers the apostrophe before the *s*.

> the 1960s
> the 1960's

━━━◆◆▸◄◆━━━

Silas Potter taught Big Jake all he knew about the mountains and all he knew about life. But he couldn't teach the big man about death, though Big Jake figured Silas knew plenty he wasn't sharing. Not that Silas Potter was disinclined, but that there were things even Silas could not explain.

One night at the campfire, with the heavens arched dark and cold between the wide, dark treetops, Silas Potter came as close as he ever would to telling it. "A life ain't nothin' fancy nor high flung, Jake—just somethin' a man has to get through. Hopefully, at the end of it, a man's not too broken down that he's meaner for having lived. Being born and dying are the easy parts. It's the in-between that breaks a man's heart and spirit. Been that way since the first man walked the earth. That's why life's best when it's brief. When all a man expects is a short life, he keeps the important things honed sharp, both coming into the world and going out. Thinkin' it deeper than that ain't gonna change none of it."

That was about as much as Silas wanted to say on the subject.

━━━◆◆▸◄◆━━━

## *Writing Time*

You may write 2:45 a.m., 8:20 A.M, 3:17 p.m., or 6:30 P.M., but not in text. Why? Because your reader will know you are being lazy. When you have the advantage of text, use it, and write out what you mean.

> Incorrect: The pow wow was set for eight a.m.
>
> Correct: The pow wow was set for eight that morning. (Or *eight in the morning.*)

> Incorrect: In the a.m. we gathered to assess the threat.
>
> Correct: The next morning we gathered to assess the threat.

## *Writing Fractions*

When a fraction is the subject of a sentence and the fraction is written out, the verb must agree with the object of its following prepositional phrase. What do you mean? What's that mean? Now don't get testy, crittur. Look at the two sentences below. *Three-fourths* is the subject of both sentences, yet we need a plural verb in one sentence and a singular verb in the other.

> Three-fourths of his pelts were prime. (The prepositional phrase is *of his pelts*. The verb *were* is plural to agree with the object of the preposition (*pelts*) which is plural.)

Three-fourths of his time was spent trapping. (*Of* is the preposition. *Time* is the object of the preposition. *Time* is singular; hence, the singular verb *was*.)

When *one* is the subject of a sentence followed by a fraction, use a singular verb in agreement.

One and a half miles was a long trek over that rugged terrain.

One and a quarter pounds of sugar was a luxury to a mountain man.

---

Silas Potter was friend, mentor, and at times protector of the younger Jake McLaughlin. He freely shared his knowledge of the mountains, of trapping, hunting, horses, Indians, and survival. About the last thing Silas Potter taught Big Jake was tracking—real tracking.

"There is only one way to track," Silas told him. "A crittur has to get down into the dirt and wear out the knees of his leggings. Every creature that walks the earth leaves tracks, even some that fly and swim. If you're a tracker, you can track anything. You can track an ant across a solid rock ledge. You can track a man and tell by his tracks whether he's right handed or left handed and to which side he parts his hair. You can tell if he's carrying a rifle. You can tell how old he is, how tall, how much he weighs, whether he's Injun, white, or half-breed. You can follow a track through a dark forest on a starless night just by the gentle touch of your fingertips on the earth. You can track a man through the night and into the morning and follow his trail through the tall grass just by the darkness and shine of the first morning dew in the first light of day.

"Folks don't believe you when you tell them all this—leastwise, folks who never got down on the earth and wore out their knees and dirtied their hands and did any real tracking. What you don't tell folks—what you cannot tell them because they would never believe you—is that most times, down there in the dirt, scanning the sunlight and shadows and the lay of the land, watching the brush, noticing the branches and leaves high and low, touching the earth, scenting the wind, seeing, listening, tasting the morning mist, you are somehow following the spirit of what you are tracking. Sometimes the spirit is all that's there."

But Silas Potter was growing old, and Silas Potter had pushed his skills and his luck about as far as any mountain man could. That season Silas Potter rode into the mountains and never returned. At spring thaw, Big Jake went looking for him. He put up his traps and searched through the remaining season and into the summer. He rode deep into the mountains, but he could not find even a cold camp where Silas Potter had been. And all the next season when he was in the high country trapping along some beaver creek, or at a beaver dam, Big Jake was still searching for Silas Potter. He searched along the creeks and canyons. He spoke with Indians. He spoke with the trees and the waters and the blowing grasses. He searched the ground, he sniffed the air.

Big Jake never found any sign of his best friend, or any tracks. There was only the wind through the trees.

---

## COMMAS

Do not be afraid of commas, crittur. The comma is your friend. Like any true friend, a comma will forgive your minor transgressions.

Clarity is the principal standard for comma usage. You may omit commas that should be there, and put commas where they aren't needed—if your intentions are good. Your writing will not always be better for your good intentions, but keeping things clear will stand you in good stead.

Use commas to clarify meaning, especially when repetition or placement of words can be confusing.

> When he said shoot, shoot I did.
> Once you shoot, Locoweed Louie will set
> fire to the wagons.

Use commas to indicate words have been omitted. Don't be afraid to use semicolons to help the process along.

> Big Jake always said, if you don't know a lot
> of big words, four letter ones get your
> point across.

Sober, Big Jake would go bare-handed against grizzly bears, cougars, Indians, rattlesnakes, and tornadoes; with a few drinks in him, Iron Skillet herself.

When you argue anything with Big Jake, be ready to punch and kick and bite and gouge and thump heads; if things get really heated, be ready to fight.

Use commas to compare and contrast.

If you are going to judge Big Jake, give him lots of room. He's a mountain man, not a missionary.

Think twice, shoot once.

When uncertain, shoot once, when certain, let 'em have it all.

Use a comma between words in a series when only one conjunction is used. Place the comma before the conjunction. Do not use a comma after the last word in the series.

Big Jake McLaughlin was not interested in starting an Indian war, getting every trapper in the area killed, or getting his own scalp lifted by some hooched-up renegades. He broke out the side of the hogshead and let the whiskey spill out onto the earth, but not before he took a skin of the stuff for himself. He cleared out in a hurry, just as the war

> party of Blackfeet came riding over the
> hill.

Now it should be mentioned here that in words in a series, modern usage sometimes calls for the omission of the last comma before the conjunction. Such usage is an abomination to the writer whose goal is precision and clarity. In the first sentence below, omission of the last comma may distort the meaning. Was the horse sleek—and also fast and sure-footed in the high country? Or, as the second sentence correctly states, was the horse, sleek, fast—and also sure-footed in the high country?

> The horse was sleek, fast and sure-footed in
> the high country.
> The horse was sleek, fast, and sure-footed
> in the high country.

Do not use commas between words in a series if all the words in the series are separated by *and* or *or*.

> He built a fire and rolled out his blanket and
> went to sleep beneath the stars.
> He was cold and wet and scared and lonely.
> He was not a mountain man.
> He was cold and wet, but he wasn't scared
> or lonely. He was a mountain man.

Use a comma between pairs of adjectives separated by *and* or *or*.

> Cold and wet, scared or lonely, he was a mountain man.

Use a comma before the conjunction when the conjunction joins two independent clauses into one compound sentence. Remember, an independent clause has a subject and verb and makes enough sense to stand on its own as a complete sentence.

Remember, too, that in the heyday of the mountain man, Hawken made the finest flintlock available. Knowing that may not help a crittur with grammar, but it lends some understanding to the compound sentence in the first example below.

> A Hawken was a flintlock rife, but not every flintlock was a Hawken.
>
> He was a man of dubious repute, and that's what made him a mountain man.
>
> Big Jake loved Calls Down the Stars, and he loved being in love with her. That distinction may not make much sense to the average man, but it was all clear to Big Jake wandering alone in the mountains thinking of her.

Use commas between two or more adjectives that equally describe the same noun.

> He was a mean, dirty dude with a mean, dirty dog walking by his side.

Set off nonrestrictive appositives with commas, as in the first sentence below. In the other examples, no commas are used because the appositives are restrictive; that is, the appositives are an integral part of the sentence, without which the sentence would not convey the intended meaning.

> Our friend, Big Jake, was a good man.
> Naked and barefoot, mountain man John Colter outran his Indian pursuers.
> We the people...
> Jack the Ripper...
> Pete the Hugger...
> The poet William Butler Yeats...

(See Appositives.)

Do not use a comma between a subject and its verb. Do not use a comma between an action verb and its object, or between a linking verb and its predicate noun, predicate pronoun, or predicate adjective. Yes, of course, crittur, you may use commas for compound objects in a series and predicate nouns and predicate adjectives in a series. That was a good question, though—shows you're thinking. Just don't overdo it.

Now, pay attention, crittur, because I am about to offer up some very incorrect examples of how to use commas. Actually, they are correct examples of how not to use commas. Follow me here—and don't overdo the thinking.

Big Jake and Stinky Petey, found the skeleton of a trapper who had gotten both his hands locked in the jaws of a bear trap he was setting. (Incorrect: No comma is needed between the subject and verb.)

Big Jake and Stinky Petey were, a bit shaken. (Incorrect: No comma is needed between the linking verb and the predicate adjective.)

There wasn't much they could do for the trapper but they buried his remains and retrieved the trap for themselves. The poor coon, had no more need of it. (Incorrect: In the first sentence, the comma is needed before the conjunction *but*. The comma in the second sentence is not needed between the subject and verb.)

Use commas when you write civilian style dates. If you write the date in the military fashion, which this author prefers for its unmistakable clarity, you do not need the commas.

His birthday of May 17, 1809, was a significant date in his life.

His birthday of 19 May 1804 remained a significant date in his life, eclipsed only by 7 February 1864 when he died. (Actually, some timid of heart grammarians might think long and hard about placing a comma after the years 1804 and 1864. Not I...)

Military abbreviation calls for all the months to have but three letters and no period.

10 Mar 69
26 Aug 70
1 Nov 71 (or 01 Nov 71)
27 Sep 75
13 Sep 76

Use a comma to set off nouns in direct address.

With you as a friend, Parker Daniels, a man's got nothing to lose.
Woman, you know it's the right thing to do.
That's what I believe, Stinky Petey.

Use a comma to set off the actual words of a speaker in direct quotes. Do not use a comma before a paraphrased or indirect quote.

Big Jake yelled out, "Katie, bar the door!"
Parker Daniels said they'd never take him alive. (But in the end, he didn't put up much of a fight.)

Use a comma to set off introductory words or interjections. Use a comma to set off *yes* and *no* when *yes* or *no* begins a sentence.

> Wagh, he was some, all right, he was!
> No, I wasn't talkin' 'bout chu, Soft-Headed Sylvester.

Use a comma after an introductory subordinate clause.

> Before you go out after Old Ephraim, you'd better pack enough gun. (Thanks to author Robert Ruark for that paraphrased quote.)
> Though that wildcat weighed no more than twenty pounds, it was one hellacious fighter.

## Omitting and Adding Commas

As important as knowing when to use a comma is knowing when not to use one. If your sentence is short, you probably don't need the comma. As with wooing and wit, the end result is lost as the words are drawn out. So, as long as your sentence is not confusing, and as long as the clauses fit together logically, you may omit the comma between short independent clauses and after a short introductory phrase.

> In camp we had a fire going.
> Keep your powder dry and you'll be all right.
> Know your friends and know your enemies.

In life and in grammar, there are exceptions to most rules. Most critturs who manage to stay on the right side of things have learned when the exceptions apply and when they don't. So, there's a tad more to consider about commas and short sentences.

Now it's true, a comma alone cannot correct a run-on sentence. To correct a run-on sentence, you need a period, a comma and a conjunction, or a semi-colon between the independent clauses. That's the rule. But realistically, and in historical usage, a comma alone may join two independent clauses if the clauses are short and related, or when the tone is casual, folksy, or conversational.

> I avoided her, she was trouble.
> Nothing ventured, nothing gained.
> I came, I saw, I conquered.
> The gate went up, the ponies bolted, the chase was on.

## Commas in Other Usage

Use a comma to set off words or groups of words that interrupt the flow of the sentence.

> He was some mean looking dude, I'm here to tell you, when he walked into town wearing nothing but a Green River knife and a scowl.

Use a comma to set off *too* when *too* means "also."

> He was a trapper, too.
> He, too, was a trapper.

Use a comma when names are inverted in alphabetical lists, bibliographies, etc.

> Colter, John
> Hickok, James B.

Of course, you remember about commas setting off adjective phrases that are restrictive or nonrestrictive. I know you remember this, crittur. Don't make me repeat myself. But maybe I didn't mention that when an adjective clause or adjective phrase comes at the end of a sentence, a comma is generally not used.

> We crossed several creeks, *which were swollen with runoff,* as a warring band of Blackfeet took up our tracks.
> The creek *that almost swept us away* ran cold and fast.
> The Hawken was a rifle *of exceptional quality.*

## *Cities, States, and Zip Codes*

Use commas to set off cities and states from the rest of the sentence. The only reason why this is a rule is because people with insufficient brain cells would get confused without the comma after the state. There could be no other logic for this stupid rule which is widely accepted both east and west of the Mississippi River.

> He was born not far from New Orleans, Louisiana, in a thicket along the Natchez Trace.

Do not use a comma between the state and zip code, but use two spaces between them on the keyboard. Use the U.S. Postal Service two letter abbreviation (two capital letters) on your envelope; spell out the state on the letter inside.

> Address on the inside of the letter:
> Mr. Jason Pew
> 36 Shadow Ridge Drive
> Ashland, Montana  59003

> Address on the outside of the envelope:
> Ashland, MT  59003

## SEMICOLON

Use a semicolon between the elements of long compound sentences with many commas, or to designate things in a series when commas alone would be confusing.

> Big Jake's friends were there. There was Stinky Petey, a liar, a thief, a drunkard, and a snake; Soft-Headed Sylvester, a horse thief, a rake, and a cad; Zeke Hatcher, a smiling, happy-go-lucky no-account double-crosser lying in the weeds for the first opportunity to do you

in; Parker Daniels, a womanizer, a four-flusher, a coward, and a cold-hearted swindler who'd steal your poke and shoot you in the back if ever he got half a chance. They were Big Jake's friends because none of any of that mattered to Big Jake as long as he never left himself open to be hurt by them. He enjoyed sitting back and watching them get themselves in and out of the most gol-durndest situations.

The mountain man endured mosquitoes, gnats, chiggers, ticks, leeches, and snakes; fought off hostile Indians, grizzly bears, an occasional cougar, or maybe a rabid wolf; lived with heat, cold, and flood. But the mountain man was free and as wild as the winds that blew across the snow-crusted Rockies.

Use a semicolon to separate the independent clauses of a compound sentence when you do not use a conjunction.

Stalking a grizzly can be a dicey enterprise; quite often the grizzly is the one doing the stalking.

You may join two independent clauses with a conjunctive adverb if you place a semicolon before, and a comma after the conjunctive adverb. Simply inserting a conjunctive adverb between commas is incorrect.

(See Conjunctive Adverbs.)

> To shoot a rifle accurately, most trappers aimed carefully; however, Locoweed Louie hated to see violence; so, he closed his eyes, turned his head, and pulled the trigger. Sometimes the results were surprising.

Words such as *namely, for example,* or *that is* tend to weaken crisp, clean, powerful writing. If you must use them, use a semicolon preceding them.

> Parker Daniels was reasonably sure of only three critturs who didn't want to see him hanged that day; namely, Zeke Hatcher, Soft-Headed Sylvester, and Big Jake McLaughlin—and they all hated him.
>
> "You're my best friend," Parker Daniels implored Big Jake.
>
> "You poor crittur," Big Jake mumbled under his breath.

## USING QUOTATION MARKS

The best way to learn how to use quotation marks is to observe carefully how it's done in good books. But even some good writers in some very fine publications make some horrendous mistakes with quotations and dialogue. So, let's point out some general rules to keep us out of high water.

## Rule #1

Know the difference between a direct quote and an indirect quote or paraphrase. A direct quote is the actual, exact words a person speaks. Direct quotes must be set off with quotation marks. But when you paraphrase what a person says, you do not use quotation marks unless you want to be sure the reader knows certain words are not yours.

In the last example below, you want the reader to know that Locoweed Louie called the Indians "stinkin' Injuns," and that those are not your words. In fact, you know more clean Indians than clean mountain men.

> Locoweed Louie closed his eyes, turned his head, pointed his rifle, and said, "I gotcha covered, you stinkin' Injuns!" (Exact quote)
>
> Locoweed Louie told the Indians he had them covered. (Paraphrased, no quotation marks)
>
> Locoweed Louie said he had the "stinkin' Injuns" covered. (You find his exact words offensive, so you put them in quotes to tell the reader as much about Locoweed Louie as about the Indians.)

## Rule #2

The end punctuation is placed inside the quotation marks when the sentence ends with the quote.

"Why are you looking that way," Big Jake
asked Locoweed Louie, "when your rifle
is pointed the other way?"

## Rule #3

A quotation is a sentence within a sentence; so, capitalize the first letter of the first word of the quote.
And because you have a sentence within a sentence,
it is not unusual to have two end punctuations in the
sentence, as in the second example below.

Big Jake asked, "Is everythin' you said,
everythin' you know, Locoweed Louie?"
"Is anybody believing me?" cried Locoweed
Louie.

## Rule #4

Most times a comma sets off the quote from the
speaker of the quote, as in the first two examples
below. But in sentences where the quote comes
before the speaker and ends in a question mark or
exclamation point, the end punctuation is placed
inside the quotation marks. Now the end punctuation, not the comma, sets off the quote from the
speaker.

"I knows there's Indians real close," whis-
pered Big Jake.
Soft-Headed Sylvester answered, "I'll have a
look-see."
"Keep your head down!" he hollered to Soft-
Headed Sylvester.

"Why?" asked Soft-Headed Sylvester.

## *Rule #5*

From time to time, as we speak, we quote things other people say. If, as we are speaking, we quote exactly what another person said, we have a quote inside a quote. An outer quotation mark has two dangling do-dad hook-like finger things (" "); an inner quotation mark has only one dangling do-dad hook-like finger thing (' ').

> Big Jake said, "With my own ears I heard Stinky Petey say, 'Parker Daniels is gettin' hisself run out o' town on a rail.'"

## *Rule #6*

This rule assumes a crittur has keen logic skills, which I know you do, crittur. So pay close attention. You may place an end punctuation mark outside the quotation marks if the end punctuation is not part of the quote. Say Zeke Hatcher is having a bad fur season. No, crittur, don't actually say it. Pay attention. Let's try this another way.

> "Trappin' is mighty poor this season," Zeke said.

Now, when Zeke said that, he did not ask a question. He made a statement, plain and simple. But Big Jake was there, and he heard what Zeke said, and that year Big Jake was having an exceptionally successful season. Big Jake found it hard to believe any trapper wouldn't be doing well that season in those mountains, unless he spent most of his time drinking and gambling.

The first example below is a quote inside a quote. The second example is written in narrative form. In both examples the question mark belongs outside the quote because it is Big Jake, not Zeke, who is asking the question. Remember, Zeke made a statement; Big Jake is asking a question about that statement.

> Big Jake asked incredulously, "Did Zeke say, 'Trappin' is mighty poor this season'?"
>
> Big Jake could hardly believe what he had heard. Had Zeke actually said, "Trappin' is mighty poor this season"?

## Rule #7

Use quotation marks to point out words with unusual meanings, special wink-of-the-eye connotations between the writer and the reader, or to indicate misnomers.

> If you told Soft-Headed Sylvester you wanted to introduce him to a woman who had lots of "personality," he'd figure she must be mighty ugly. On the other hand, women, after meeting Soft-Headed Sylvester, considered him "different," with an "interesting" face—like a shaggy dog with its backside shaved, walking backward.

# HYPHENS

*The United Press International (UPI) Stylebook* offers some excellent examples and clearly explained rules regarding when to hyphenate and when to resist the temptation. In similar fashion, Patricia O'Conner in *Woe is I* and Jan Venolia in *Write Right!* tackle hyphens with simple, pure logic. You can live by any of those books, crittur, and do all right for yourself. But for this section, I have gleaned and bundled, tested and confirmed, and with a few thrown-in tricks of my own, I offer the following.

Now, personally, I do not like hyphens. I don't trust them. In this section I am not talking about hyphens that break off words at the end of a line. I'm talking about hyphens in compound words.

Some words are always hyphenated. They are the easy ones. You will find those words in any good dictionary. But not every dictionary has an entry for words such as *president-elect*.

Many compound words are not always hyphenated. But, be fearless, crittur. I've broken it down into three basic rules that will gratify and satisfy.

## *Rule #1 (Hyphens and Nouns, Adverbs and Adjectives)*

Hyphenate a compound adjective before a noun. Do not hyphenate after a noun.

> The board of directors of a business can talk about either their *first-year* profits or profits in their *first year*.

He was a well-trained horse. The horse was well trained.

Do not hyphenate when the compound word includes the word *very* or an adverb ending in *ly*.

He was a highly trained horse. He was a very well trained horse.

This rule includes common phrases. In the first part of the examples below, *hand to hand* and *one on one* are adverbs. In the second part of the examples, they are adjectives coming before nouns, and therefore, they are hyphenated.

They battled hand to hand. It was a hand-to-hand battle.
They met one on one. It was a one-on-one meeting.

## Rule #2 (Clarity and Common Sense)

Use a hyphen for clarity. You can *recount* a tale, or you can *re-count* money. You can make a *remark*, or you can *re-mark* the trail. And how else would you write about *tax-breaks* without the hyphen?

By the time he showered her father and all her relatives with gifts, a mountain man was painfully reminded that being a squaw-man was an expensive proposition.

### *Rule #3 (Hyphens and Compound Adjectives)*

Use a hyphen for a compound adjective when the adjective stands alone as a specific concept.

As always, *UPI* comes up with great examples: *soft-spoken*, *self-appointed*, and *quick-witted*. But just so a simple mountain crittur can understand, I've come up with the following:

> Kit Carson was wilderness-smart.
> Kit Carson was a well-respected mountain man.

## CAPITALIZATION

Capital letters are pretty simple and fall into some well-defined areas. I believe I have them all listed below, but if there are any areas I'm leaving out, they probably aren't important anyway. Basically, use a capital letter:

★ to begin a sentence.

★ to name the months of the year and the days of the week, but not the seasons.

★ for holidays and special commemorations.

★ to begin the first word in the greeting and salutation of a friendly or business letter.

★ for the first word and all important words in the titles of books, stories, and poems.

★ for the first word in a direct quotation.

★ for titles of respect and honor before a name.

★ for all proper nouns and proper adjectives.

# Punctuation

## Periods

Use a period after all declarative and most imperative sentences. Use periods for initials and abbreviations. Use periods for abbreviated titles such as Mr. and Mrs.

## Abbreviations

Abbreviations that are shortened words require a period (Nov., Fri., Fra., Ger., Assoc.). Acronyms and abbreviations that require several words do not always require periods (AFL-CIO, NAACP, NASA, CORE, NBC, IBM).

When acronyms and abbreviations take possessive form, however, they do not always like an apostrophe and *s*. Instead of writing *IBM's products*, you may want to write: *IBM products*.

B.C. means *before Christ*. A.D. (Lat. anno Domini) means *in the year of our Lord*, or *in the year of the Lord*, and signifies all the years after the birth of Jesus.

When you use B.C., use it after the year. Use A.D. before the year.

> Julius Caesar was killed in 44 B.C.
>
> In A.D. 1492, Columbus discovered America. He also discovered the Indians.

## Exclamation Points

Use an exclamation point to set off an introductory word or an interjection that conveys urgency, surprise, joy, anguish, or relief.

"Hey! What are you doing here?" asked Big
    Jake.

"Whoa! Big Jake, are you sticking beans up
    your nose?"

"So, what's it to you?"

"Hoboy!"

---

Big Jake knew the power of simple words spoken
quietly. One time—one of the few times he was ever
in Independence, Missouri—Big Jake happened to
turn a street corner where he encountered a pretty
city lady, in city garb, trying to buy a spirited stallion
from a trader who had too much savvy and too much
probity to sell so much horse to so little a woman.

"I am heading for the mountains, and that is the
horse that is going to take me, and, mister, you are
going to sell him to me because my money is as good
as anybody else's money!" the woman said hotly.

"I told you, lady, the horse ain't for sale."

"The sign says otherwise."

"The sign's wrong."

"Contract law says, that sign is an offer to sell and
I…"

"Here in Independence, lady, there ain't no law.
Anyway, the sign's wrong."

"Then my fist smashing your mouth is going to
decide what that sign says."

"The horse ain't for sale, lady—not to you."

It was a cool morning, the air clean with the smell
of horses, and Big Jake found himself standing there

unabashedly listening to this conversation and smiling broadly waiting for the city lady to clobber the horse trader. He would have paid admission to see that. The big guy liked this woman trimmed and proper in the latest cut of city fashion. He admired her pluck. She was a small, soft woman, who looked bony enough to be dangerous. She had expressive eyes and high cheekbones, and she stood close to the ground, lithe and petite and pretty.

She had pluck, all right. Big Jake liked the way her stick floated in the current, and he warmed to her immediately. And she knew her horseflesh. At the far end of the corral, the big stallion the woman wanted stood handsomely in the shadows of the tall shade trees. The stallion was probably the finest animal the trader had to offer—a stout and hearty dark chestnut that could take a man or a woman clear to Califor-nigh-a and back again. Big Jake watched as the big horse ambled out into the morning sunlight tossing its handsome head and its huge neck.

Now Big Jake could have solved the entire controversy by simply buying the horse for the lady. But watching the exchange between the woman and the horse trader was just too much fun to pass up. The trader was going to lose against this woman—Big Jake would have taken odds on that.

Finally, in sheer desperation, the woman gritted her teeth, balled up her fist, and swung from her ankles. Now Big Jake loved a brawl, and he especially loved a "cat fight" when two women got down and at it, so this was fair sport for him. But for some perverse reason uncharacteristic of him, the big man caught the woman's hand mid-arc before it made contact with the trader's nose. In a lightning flash, her other fist swung around and smashed the grin off Big Jake's face. That buckled his knees and got the big guy's attention and brought the trader to smiling—albeit after he had stepped back a couple of paces. Right about now Big Jake's liking this woman was wearing thin.

"Back off, you big ass!" she shouted in Big Jake's face, and the big man wisely let loose her hand and backed away.

Now at this point it's difficult to tell whether it was Big Jake's simple words spoken quietly that saved the day. That's how it's been told, anyway, but somewhere after Big Jake's, "Hold on—hold off—calm down, lady!" the mountain man offered a simple, quiet suggestion to the horse trader.

"Sell the horse to the lady," Big Jake said calmly, evenly.

"You're nuts!"

"Sell the horse to the lady," Big Jake repeated.

The horse trader considered all of two seconds before answering. "All right—she can have her damned horse!"

"Don't you use that language in the presence of a lady!" the woman shouted. "You apologize or you're going to be picking yourself up out of a pile of horse dung!"

"Apologize to the lady," Big Jake said. Again his voice was calm.

"Why...why!" The trader looked at Big Jake and then at the lady and then back at Big Jake before he continued. "Why…Why, I'm sorry. I'm right sorry, lady."

The woman took a deep breath of self-satisfaction. "You may call me Mrs. Potter—Mrs. Silas Potter—and you remember my name. And as soon as I change my clothes, and gather my gear, and mount my horse here, I am off to the mountains to join my husband. And you will be lucky if he does not come back here to Independence, Missouri, to pay you a visit, Mister horse-seller."

"Yes, Ma'am," said the trader. "I mean, yes, Mrs. Potter."

But Big Jake's face had darkened as he looked at her. He shifted his weight awkwardly before he spoke. "We need to talk, Ma'am," he said simply.

"You need to get out of my way," Silas Potter's wife answered sternly. But her voice was calm now, and a warmth was beginning to glow in her manner and mood. The journey west had cost her nearly all of her money and all of her courage and she had been carrying a lot of things deep in her heart, and now, as she was getting closer to the mountains, she could feel the swell of it all coming to the surface.

"May I buy you dinner, Mrs. Potter?" Big Jake continued.

"You may not."

"Mrs. Potter…Silas was…Silas was a friend of mine, Ma'am."

Now the woman looked sharply at the big man before her. Her nostrils flared for breath, and she pulled her lips tight so that the words would not ask the question. But it was a question she didn't have to ask. She closed her eyes and the prettiness of her face contorted as she steeled herself against an invisible flood sweeping over her.

Big Jake could feel something tighten and then rip deep inside his chest. He looked away to the big chestnut stallion as it crossed again to the far end of the corral and stood in the cool dappled sunlight of the shade trees. The animal had stamina, strength, and spirit. The big horse looked back at him and tossed its powerful neck and snorted. Silas Potter's woman had come a long way to Independence, Missouri, to buy a fine horse she wouldn't need.

---

## DOUBLE NEGATIVES

Remember your math teacher telling you that two negatives make a positive? It's the same in American grammar. If you say, "I didn't eat nuthin'," you are saying you ate something. Think of it conceptually. The concept of "eat nothing" means you went without food. By saying you didn't eat nothing, you are saying you didn't go without food; that is, you really ate something.

When you say, "I didn't hit nobody," you are saying you hit somebody. Think of the concept of "hitting nobody." You kept your hands to yourself. You are innocent. But that didn't happen. You didn't keep your hands to yourself. You didn't "hit nobody"—you hit somebody, you probably broke his nose, and you are in big trouble.

Anyway, avoid double negatives. And be careful of words that you may not ordinarily think of as negative. The following are some of the many negative words to keep in mind: *never, neither, nor, hardly, scarcely, nothing, nowhere*. So, it's incorrect to say:

> I hardly never drink alcohol.
> The avoidance of war was forestalled.

Some double negatives are perfectly all right.

> Big Jake is not untruthful, he's just untactful.
> It is not intolerable.
> I don't believe you didn't load your gun.
> Sagebrush Sam is not without his faults.
> It's nothing you can't handle.

Other double negatives are downright confusing and need to be recast.

> Confusing: They couldn't believe he was not unprepared.
> Better: They couldn't believe he was prepared.

We've almost to the last mountain range, crittur. You're doing fine. I hereby confer upon you the title of:

## ✳ SAVANT OF STYLE ✳

# Usage and Stuff to Make Others Think You're Smart:

---

### The Fancy, Foofaraw Stuff

---

*"To live on the wind is never to die."*

⟨SILAS POTTER⟩

## USAGE—THE TRICKY STUFF

Big Jake wore his Green River knife on his belt, keen edged and at the ready. He carried a fine Hawken rifle and knew how to use it. These were the tools of his trade, crittur, just as you need your arsenal of words and the skills to use them correctly. You'll get some of that in this final section, but you'll need to go out and learn more than what's in this book. Teachers can walk with us only so far. Then they step aside, and we go on alone carrying only their words and their memory. Go out and get yourself a good dictionary, crittur, and some of the reference books listed in the bibliography at the end of this book.

You do this grammar thing right, crittur—not by half. Then, like Big Jake, you'll have something to reach for when times get dicey. Then, like Big Jake, you can spend your evenings by the fireside with your pipe, a jug of whiskey, and a quiet mind. All things considered, a man can't want for better than that. Maybe a good woman by his side to gently enlighten him when he's being an ass.

For this last section, I have consulted most of the invaluable publications listed in the Bibliography (page 341). I have tried to glean the best from them and put it all together into a clear, concise compilation of genius and educated risk-taking.

In reading this last section, crittur, remember: words designated as "nonstandard" are slang words. Nonstandard words should not be used except for effect or in dialogue to add realism and local flavor. Remember, too, if words are said to be "informal," they should not be used in formal writing. All right, let's begin.

### *a lot* vs *alot*
*A lot* is informal, but *alot* as one word is dead wrong incorrect. *A lot* is all right, but don't use it a lot, and not at all in formal writing.

> Many (not a lot of) people think that's wrong.

### *a while*, *awhile*, *while*

*A while* denotes an unspecified short period of time. If you use the noun phrase *a while*, you may or may not use the preposition *for*.

> He lingered a short (or long) while.
> He lingered for a short (or long) while.

*Awhile* indicates an indefinite duration of time. When you use *awhile*, the preposition *for* is understood and should be omitted.

> The trappers worked the icy stream awhile.
> The trappers worked the icy stream for a while.

*While* used alone means to spend time pleasantly, or indicates something happening at the same time another thing is happening.

> While he smoked his pipe for a while, he sat awhile and whiled away his time.

*While* can be a conjunction implying the contrary or meaning *although* or *even though*.

> While Big Jake proposed marriage that night, he intended to be long gone by morning.

### *abstract* vs *abstracted*

*Abstract* means envisioned or comprehended apart from actuality, reality, or a tangible object; theoretical. Also, an abstract can be a summary of a statement or passage.

Abstracted means preoccupied, deeply engrossed, lost in thought, apart from something.

### *accept* vs *except*

To *accept* is to agree to a condition, to accede to something, or to willingly receive something offered by another. *Except* means to exclude from consideration, etc.

### *adverse* vs *averse*

*Adverse* means opposing or thwarting a purpose or intent. *Averse* means disinclined, opposed, unwilling, loath to do something

> He was averse to venturing outdoors in adverse conditions.

### *advice* vs *advise*

*Advice* is a noun. *Advice* is an opinion or recommendation given or offered to another, usually as helpful guidance. *Advise* is a verb. *Advise* is the act of giving or offering advice.

> You can advise Big Jake, but chances are he won't take your advice.

### *affect* vs *effect*

*Affect* is a verb meaning to influence.

> Big Jake was genuinely affected by Sagebrush Sam's tears, but not enough so as to return his squaw. He wasn't exactly sure whether Sagebrush Sam's tears were tears of grief at forever losing his woman, or tears of joy at finally losing his woman.

*Affect* can mean to feign, to give or assume a false appearance.

> Later, Sagebrush Sam affected an air of indifference about the whole affair.

*Effect* can be a verb meaning to cause.

> Iron Skillet was known to effect a positive improvement in Big Jake's manners each time she connected with her iron fry pan at the end of a wide arcing round house swing to his head.

*Effect* can be a noun meaning result.

> An arrow is of little effect against an angry grizzly unless it is a well-placed arrow.

### *afterward* vs *afterwards*

In American grammar, we do not use *afterwards*. The British may love it, but remember, we kicked their butts in the Revolution and in Mr. Madison's War, and we chased them into Canada and beyond the Pacific coast.

### *all ready* vs *already*

*All ready* means, you are ready. You are all—every bit of you—ready, prepared for some eventuality, or inclined or disposed to do something. *Already* means *previous* or *so soon*.

Are you all ready already, Wiley Willie?

### *all right* vs *alright*

*All right* means safe and secure; it means an affirmative "yes," or indicates something is satisfactory. *Alright* is nonstandard. *Alright* is never all right.

### *all together* vs *altogether*

*All together* is used to indicate a gathering. *Altogether* means totally or entirely.

The trappers were all together in camp that day. When the squall kicked up they were altogether drenched.

### *allude (allusion)*, *elude (elusive)*, *illusion, delusion*, *refer, revert*

To *allude* to something is to intimate, to hint or make an oblique, unspecified connection or relationship to.

(Usually used when the source is not stated. Otherwise, *refer* is preferable.)

> He did not get into specifics; he just alluded in general to Indian lore, tribal secrets, and ghosts around the campfire.
>
> In an even voice he commented that walking past a burial ground on a late autumn night was not advisable. It was an unmistakable allusion I took to heart.

To *refer* or *make reference to* is to be more specific.

> He referred me to Jim Bridger.
>
> When we talked of attacking the Sioux, he reminded us of the Little Big Horn, a reference to Custer's foolhardy arrogance.

The word *revert* should never be followed by *back* because *revert* can only mean *back*. Writing "revert back" is a redundancy.

*Refer* is different. The term *refer back* is not always redundant. Sometimes you may need to *refer ahead*, and if you can refer ahead as well as back, you may need to make the distinction. If your sentence is clear just using *refer*, omit *back* or *ahead*.

> Refer to this section when needed.

To *elude* means to flee, evade, escape. *Elusive* (the tendency to elude) indicates something fleeting, transitory, indefinite, or nondescript, such as an elusive dream.

An *illusion* is an incorrect perception of reality, the act of being fooled by a misconception.

> The Donner Party suffered under the illusion that man could master the mountains.

*Delude* suggests something more sinister, a deliberate deception. *Delusion* is a misguided belief, sometimes as a result of mental illness.

> Delusions of ghosts tormented his fevered delirium.

### *also* vs *too*

Unless the word *also* begins a sentence as an introductory word, you do not need to set it off with a comma. But you need commas to set off the word *too* anywhere in a sentence where you use *too* to mean *also*.

> He also was a mountain man of some renown. (He, like Jim Bridger, was well known and respected.)
>
> He was also a mountain man of some renown. (In addition to his other talents, he was a mountain man, well known and respected.)
>
> He, too, was a mountain man of some renown.
>
> Also, he was a trapper and guide.

He was a trapper and guide, too.
(See **to, too, two**.)

## *ameliorate* vs *help*

*Help* suggests a quick and limited improvement to a vexing problem. *Ameliorate* means to improve in a way that is general and cannot be measured. To ameliorate is to improve a pervasive condition sorely in need of change.

Making Stinky Petey wash his socks helped make cabin life a little more tolerable.

The blankets and emergency food and medical supplies ameliorated the hunger and sickness on the Sioux Reservation.

## *among* vs *between*

The old rule is, you use *between* when referring to two people (or things) and *among* when referring to three or more:

They divided the gun powder between Big Jake and Jedediah Smith.

They divided the plunder among the three men.

A discerning speaker or writer, however, learns quickly to abandon the old rule when writing such sentences as:

Young Jedediah Smith had gone under to a band of Comanches on the Cimarron,

> but not before he had explored and mapped much of the country between Independence, Missouri, California, Mexico, and the Columbia River.

You are safe to use *between* when the components of your sentence are equal and are clearly designated (when individual entities are essential to your meaning), and *among* when the components are vague (or when individual entities are not important).

> Jim Bridger visited among the Cheyenne and Crow. He walked the well-trodden grass between the many tepees and listened to the talk of the women. Among the braves, he sensed a growing resentment toward the white man. Still, he was able to negotiate an informal peace pact between the trappers, the cavalry, and the Indians.

### *anal* vs *annals*

> Big Jake will go down in the annals of history. (Please spell it with two *n*'s.)

### *any more* vs *anymore*

*Any more*, written as two words, means anything additional. *Anymore*, as one word, is an informal adverb meaning now or currently. *Anymore* usually has negative connotations.

He hasn't friends anymore since he hasn't any more money.

In some western areas of the country, anymore means nowadays. It is difficult to explain the subtle difference here except to give an example of the word in the middle of a sentence.

It's a shame anymore how kids don't listen.

### *any one* vs *anyone*

(See **every one** vs **everyone**.)

*Any one* is an adjective-pronoun combination indicating any single indefinite one. Usually the preposition *of* or a noun follows *any one*.

*Anyone* is a pronoun synonymous with the personal pronoun *anybody*. If you are not sure whether to use *any one* or *anyone*, consider the following as a guide: If you can replace *any one* with *anybody*, you probably want to use *anyone* instead.

Any one of us can whoop your butt, Big Jake. (This is correct because you cannot say: "Anybody of us...")

Any one trapper is worth twenty sodbusters. (This is correct because you cannot say: "Anybody trapper...")

Anyone can easily mistake Big Jake for a mangy old bear. (This is correct because here you can say: "Anybody can..." so any one as two words would be incorrect.)

Anyone may enter into the negotiations.
(Anybody and everybody may sit and
argue and discuss the issues.)

Any one may enter into the negotiations.
(Any one person—and only one—of a certain group of persons may sit and parley.)

### anyplace vs anywhere
*Anyplace* is an informal adverb. Use *anywhere*.

### any way vs anyway
*Any way* as two words means "in any manner."
*Anyway* as one word means *anyhow* or *under any
circumstances*. *Anyways* (with an *s*) is just plain
unacceptable at all times. Even in story dialogue,
only low-lifes use *anyways*.

If by insisting on using my own deck of
cards, I in any way impugned your reputation, Four-flusher Phil, please feel free
to shuffle the deck anyway you like.

Is there any way in particular we should run
you out of camp, Four-flusher Phil—
'cause we never trusted you anyway.

"We's gonna run ya outta camp anyways,"
said Zeke Hatcher.

Women love their men the best they can, with all
they have within them. There's a lot of "toleratin'" on
their part, bless their hearts.

That's as good as it's ever going to get. A man who
knows the way the stick floats can abide that kind of

love. He is what he is, and sometimes that's all he can be. He loves his women with his whole heart, and tolerates her, too. It's not a bad arrangement.

### *anxious* vs *anxious*

If you are anxious *for* something, it's usually a positive thing. It means you are eager for it. If you are anxious *about* something, it is usually negative. It means you are worried and concerned about it.

### *appose* vs *oppose*

*Appose* means to juxtapose or place next to something. Unlike almost every other animal, humans have apposable thumbs that work opposite their other four fingers to allow them to grip weapons and tools. Still, claws and fangs are sometimes preferable.

*Oppose* means to contend with, to compete against, to be in opposition to.

> Before you oppose states' rights, you'd better understand it's the backbone of our constitution.

### *appraise, apprise, apprize*

*Appraise* means to establish the worth or value of something or estimate its nature, essence, or quality. *Apprise* means to inform or notify another. *Apprize* is used in the sense you apprize or appreciate the worth of something. In modern usage it is probably best not to use *apprize* lest folks think you misspelled the word or you're a Brit or something.

The assayer appraised the gold nugget and apprised the prospector of its worth.

### *as* vs *like*

*As* is a preposition and a conjunction; *like* is a preposition followed by an object. Generally, do not use *like* as a conjunction except in informal writing. Use *as* before a phrase or clause and before a verb. Before using *like* as a conjunction, consider instead using *as*, *as if*, or *as though*.

> Incorrect: Like I was saying…
> Correct: As I was saying…

> Incorrect: He sat before the fire and ate his charred buffalo meat like the caveman had done thousands of years earlier.
> Correct: He sat before the fire and ate his charred buffalo meat as the caveman had done thousands of years earlier.

> Incorrect: He came strolling into camp like he was king of the mountain men.
> Correct: He came strolling into camp as though he were king of the mountain men.

When a time relationship is expressed, as in the first two sentences below, no comma is needed. When a cause and effect relationship or a casual reference is expressed, as in the second set of sentences, a comma should be used.

A lone wolf howled as the moon rose above the mountains.

They ran out of whiskey just as Big Jake entered camp.

Sagebrush Sam had drunk the most, as Big Jake had suspected.

There was still tobacco, as Big Jake had it hidden in a sack of dirty socks.

*As* is a conjunction when it means *that*. When *as* is a conjunction, it usually needs a verb.

I don't know *as* he's a trustworthy scout.

*As* may also mean *functioning as*.

He assumed a role *as* spokesman.

Because *like* is a preposition, it needs an object to follow it, usually a noun or pronoun. If you have a verb following *like*, you probably need to go back and change like to *as*. All of the following sentences are correct.

He fights like a grizzly.
He fights as a grizzly would fight.

He was a trapper, *like* me.
He was a trapper, *as* I was.
He was a trapper, *as* was I.

In informal writing, however, *like* may be used as a conjunction when a following verb is omitted.

> He walked into camp like a man with a purpose.

Also, in informal writing, *like* may be used as a conjunction when *as* would distract the reader by drawing attention from the meaning of the passage to the words themselves thereby disrupting the flow of the reading.

> Trappers today aren't like the old-timers were in the days of Hugh Glass and Jim Bridger. (Actually, you'd be better served here to recast this sentence with more precision: "Trappers today aren't as resourceful as they were in the days of Hugh Glass and Jim Bridger.")
>
> Trapping in Blackfeet territory in the early 1800's was like cornering an angry buffalo and then going in after him with a pocketknife to try to turn him into a steer. (It is not likely that recasting this sentence would add or detract anything.)

*As* is sometimes used incorrectly to complete certain verbs. A careful writer understands that *as* may correctly be joined to some verbs and not to others.

Correct: A steaming bowl of Big Jake's muskrat stew was regarded as culinary enchantment by Stinky Petey and the camp dogs.

Incorrect: Others considered it as inhumane to risk injuring the dogs. (Omit *as*.)

Correct: Sitting Bull was esteemed as a fearless and cunning warrior.

Incorrect: Iron Skillet was deemed as a troublesome shrew. (Omit *as*.)

Correct: Big Jake was seen as a wise, circumspect, and cowardly husband.

### *as* vs *so*

Here is where there is a clear distinction between English grammar and American grammar. In a negative context, a Brit might say: "He's not *so bad as* all that." An American would say: "He's not *as bad as* all that."

An English-speaking Canadian should query: "Is it *so far as* a kilometer?" An American-speaking American would ask: "Is it *as far as* a mile?"

An important technicality to remember: When you American critturs use your American *as* in comparison, complete the *as* component of your comparison before you go on to your second element.

Correct: The female is as deadly as, or deadlier than, the male.

> Incorrect: The female is as deadly, or dead-
> lier than, the male.

Remember: Use a comma before *as* when making a casual reference, or to express a cause and effect relationship.

> He was killed by renegade warriors, as we
> expected.

Do not use a comma before *as* when time is a factor.

> They were about to lift his scalp as I rode
> up.

### assistance *vs* assistants
*Assistance* is a noun meaning help or aid. *Assistants* is a plural noun meaning persons who assist or aid, usually in a subordinate capacity. In its singular form, assistant can be an adjective.

### assume *vs* presume
*Assume* is to make an assumption, to suppose, to accept as true for argument's sake, to take for granted, or to pretend to be something you are not.

> I assume you are a trapper.
> He assumed the airs of a wagon master.

*Presume* is similar, but more forceful. *Presume* connotes arrogance. *Presume* means to accept as true without real proof (to be presumptive), to endeavor to do a thing without the right or without permission (to be presumptuous).

Idiot! You presume to be a guide?

### *at* vs *with*
Use *at* when referring to inanimate objects; use *with* when referring to people.

> Big Jake was happy with Calls Down the Stars of the Dakota Sioux.
> He was annoyed at the perfidy of Iron Skillet of the Blackfoot.
> Big Jake was disappointed at the loss of the Rocky Mountain Fur Company. He was incensed with Bill Sublette who called in his notes and drove the company under.

**"The old have squandered the important things, and the young will do the same. The old die along the path and the young tread onward. The path is a long, wide, winding hoop."**

☞**SILAS POTTER**

### *back of*, *in back of* vs *behind*
Don't say, "he went *in back of* the cabin"; say "he went *behind* the cabin."

### back up *vs* backup

*Back up* is a verb. Back up and try it again.

*Backup* is an adjective. This is my backup shot-gun.

*Backup* is also a noun. The backup of wagons, mules, and oxen stretched for a mile along the trail.

### beside *vs* besides

*Beside* means next to. *Besides* means furthermore or in addition to.

> That night, down by the river, Wiley Willie kissed Moose-face Maggie Marlow as he sat beside her in the moonlight. Wiley Willie, it was said, was a desperate man, but he liked Moose-face Maggie's personality. Besides, not even a moose could have kissed back better than she did that night, there beneath the stars.

### bi *vs* semi

These prefixes are tough for some critturs to get straight in their heads. Use *bi* to mean a whole two or two whole numbers, and use *semi* to mean halved or cut into two. So, *biweekly* means every two weeks, *bimonthly* means every two months, *biannually* or *biyearly* means every two years. *Semiweekly* indicates something happens twice each week, *semimonthly* indicates something happens twice each month, *semiannually* indicates something happens twice each year.

### *blowup* vs *blow up*
The noun *blowup* is an explosion, a blast, a violent outburst of temper or emotion. The verb *blow up* means to explode, or to lose one's temper.

### *boar, boor, bore*
*Boar* is a wild boar, a pig that is not castrated, or the adult male of certain mammals such as the beaver or bear.

*Boor* is an ill-bred, rude oaf.

*Bore* means to tire, indicating tedium or weariness from dullness, length, slowness, or lack of stimulation.

*Bore* also means to drill into something and make a hole. (Don't forget the bore of a rifle.)

*Bore* is also the past tense of the verb *bear*.

### *cache*, *secrete*, *cloak*
*Cache* means to hide away in storage for later use. A crittur caches food and provisions from wild animals, thieving men, and other varmints. *Cache* is a noun meaning the items secreted away, or the physical structure of the cache itself; for a mountain man this is usually set high on poles or in a tree away from bears. (Wolverines, however, have little difficulty getting to and raiding a cache.)

*Secrete* is similar to cache in that the word implies concealment for a specific purpose and for later use by the one who stashed the items away. A bear secretes her cubs in her den.

*Cloak* connotes something evil or at least devious. *Cloak* means to hide something by trickery or subterfuge, by disguising it as something else, or by masking it.

> He cloaked his treacherous designs in the trappings of a smile, a slap on the back, and an offer of whiskey.

### *calumny* vs *obloquy*

*Calumny* is a generally widespread false allegation—a mean, vicious, malicious lie intended to cause harm to someone. The key word here is "false."

*Obloquy* denotes widespread public disdain, public censure, public outcry, public outrage, loss of credibility, loss of honor, loss of a good name, loss of good repute. Unlike *calumny*, *obloquy* may, in fact, be true. Plainly put, *obloquy* is a bad reputation justly or unjustly earned, possibly true or possibly false, but *obloquy* nonetheless.

(See **libel** vs **slander**.)

### *capital* vs *capitol*

*Capital* is a city or town that is the official seat of county, state, or federal government. *Capital* is also money, assets, or wealth in general. Finally, *capital* can mean something highly important, primary, or chief; hence, capital punishment. A *capital offense* is an offense punishable by death.

> It was a capital idea...
> It was a capital stroke of luck...

*Capitol* is the physical building wherein a legislature sits.

### *client* vs *customer*
If you buy a product from a shop, you are a *customer*. If you engage the professional services of a lawyer or architect, or any "one-on-one" entrepreneur—if you order something specially made from a designer, or commission an original creative work—you are a *client*.

### *compare to* vs *compare with*
You compare similar things *with* one another. You compare unlike things *to* one another.

> The bureaucracy of the Bureau of Indian Affairs may be compared with the bureaucracy of the Interior Department. The Northern Cheyenne Indians may be compared with the Crow Indians.

> Death may be compared to sleep, to a final rest; life may be compared to a journey, to a race, to a game of chance.

### *complement, compliment, complete, compleat*
*Complement* is something that makes another thing complete; a full, complete whole; something that brings another thing to wholeness or perfection.

*Compliment* is an expression of praise or admiration.

*Complete* means total.

> Big Jake was a complete ___.
> a. fool
> b. idiot
> c. ass

*Complete* is also used to indicate an absolute, as "perfection" or "primary" are absolute. But strangely, in our American logic, *complete* may be qualified.

> Jim Bridger was the most complete authority on the subject of Indians.

*Compleat* is used facetiously to mean "complete" in the archaic and literary sense of "skilled" or "accomplished."

> Henry Wells was a compleat fisherman.
> Andy Clayburne was a compleat woodsman.

> Big Jake was a compleat ___.
> a. fool
> b. idiot
> c. ass

### compose, comprise, constitute, consist, contain, include

*Compose, comprise, constitute, consist, contain, include* have various meanings. We will discuss only those meanings which tend to confuse. We'll make this simple, crittur, don't worry.

When you use the word *include*, you should follow the word with at least a partial list, and perhaps, sometimes, a full list of contents.

> Some of the Indian tribes of the northwest include the Blackfeet, Cheyenne, and Crow. (Some, but not all the tribes are mentioned here.)

Now let's get into wholes and parts of wholes. The complete whole *comprises, consists of*, is *made up of* its parts; its parts *constitute*, form, or *compose* the whole.

> An army post is comprised of commissioned officers, enlisted men, and cavalry horses. The commissioned officers, enlisted men, and cavalry horses constitute an army post.

When you use the words *comprise* or *consist of*, the reader expects a full, complete list of contents to follow. He doesn't always get it, crittur, but he expects it.

> The delegation of trappers who called on Sitting Bull *comprised* Jim Bridger, Big Jake McLaughlin, and Tom Smith. (There were these three men, and only these three men, in the delegation.)
> The Bill of Rights *comprises* the first ten amendments to the Constitution.
> The first ten amendments to the Constitution *constitute* the Bill of Rights.

### comptroller *vs* controller

Both a *comptroller* and a *controller* do the same thing—they manage the finances for a corporation—but when you give that person a title it's *comptroller*—as in "company comptroller."

### convince *vs* persuade

Use *persuade* before an infinitive. Use *convince* before a phrase.

> Fifty or so screaming Indians in war paint persuaded Big Jake to depart the area. (Big Jake was persuaded to depart...)

> The jury was convinced of his guilt.

### correspondent, corespondent, correspondence

*Correspondence* means letter writing. A professional *correspondent* is a news reporter stationed abroad or "out in the field" writing.

A *corespondent* (one *r*) co-responds sexually with another and is a codefendant in an adultery case.

### council *vs* counsel

*Counsel* can be a verb meaning to give advice to another, to recommend an action, a plan, etc.

> Big Jake, I counsel you to plead guilty and throw yourself on the mercy of Judge Hangam Hye. It sure beats facing a jury of your peers.

*Counsel* can be a noun if you take counsel in what a counselor says. Also, as a noun, *counsel* can be a lawyer.

> Will counsel for the defense approach the bench?

*Council* is a noun, a body of persons, an assembly gathered to consider and perhaps vote on various issues.

### currently *vs* presently
*Currently* is happening now, at the time that is now passing. *Presently* indicates something that will happen in a little while. Only informally does *presently* mean at the present time.

### device *vs* devise
*Device* is a noun. A device is something fashioned, made, manufactured, etc., usually for a specific purpose. A device could be a scheme or plan to effect an end result.

*Devise* is a verb. To devise something is to create it, fashion it, manufacture it, etc. One can devise a plan...devise a strategy...devise a method.

### different from *vs* different than
Use the preposition *from* instead of the conjunction *than* following *different*. The preposition *from* needs an object. The following sentences are correct.

His style is different from Zeke's style.

He is different from me.

Honor back then was different from what it is today.

A wildcat is different from a lynx.

Although *different than* is generally considered incorrect, you may get away with using it before a clause. Remember, a clause is a group of words that has its own subject and verb. So, a following verb is your clue to correct or tolerated usage.

He is different than he was in the old days.

Honor back then was different than it is today.

If you use *different than* before a clause, use it fearlessly and offer no excuses. If you are not necessarily on safe ground, at least you are on defensible ground.

### *differs from* vs *differ with*

When they disagree people differ *with* each other, but things differ, one *from* the other—that is, they are *different from* each other.

Big Jake always said his spotted dog differed from his black dog. Iron Skillet differed with him, claiming both dogs stunk to high heaven and both dogs would steal the food off your plate or the moccasins out from under your nose. (Was Big Jake sniffing his moccasins again?)

Still, the dogs differed, Big Jake insisted.

On that matter Big Jake and Iron Skillet differed.

## disburse *vs* disperse

*Disburse* is a transitive verb meaning to pay out money for salaries, expenses, etc. It makes me think of a bursar. A bursar is the treasurer of a college or the finance officer of a company.

*Disperse* is a transitive verb meaning to scatter, to spread over a wide area, to cause something to vanish, to send off (people or things) in various directions.

## discreet *vs* discrete

*Discreet* is an adjective meaning careful in speech or conduct, prudent, circumspect, tactful, judicious.

*Discrete* is an adjective meaning detached, consisting of various distinct parts, detached from others in an emotional sense.

## disingenuous, ingenuous, ingenuity

*Disingenuous* means dissembling, manipulative, crafty, not honest and straightforward.

*Ingenuous* means unsophisticated, lacking worldliness.

*Ingenuous* also means frank, honest, straightforward.

*Ingenuity* means cleverness. It connotes resourceful, intriguing cleverness.

### disinterested vs uninterested
*Disinterested* means impartial, unbiased, non-partisan, fair-minded. *Uninterested* means indifferent, not interested, not concerned.

If you were on trial for a crime, you would want a presiding judge who was disinterested, not uninterested.

### each other vs one another
Use *each other* when referring to two people or two things. Use *one another* when referring to three or more people or things.

> Big Jake and Sagebrush Sam hated each other.
>
> Zeke Hatcher, Stinky Petey, and Soft-Headed Sylvester tolerated one another.

### emigrate vs immigrate
You *emigrate* from one country and *immigrate* into another. Once you are in your new country, you are an *immigrant* from the old country. *Emigrate* is to leave; *immigrate* is to enter into.

### enthusiastic vs enthused
*Enthusiastic* denotes having a lively interest in something, favorably excited, delightfully and favorably disposed, keenly encouraged. *Enthused* is a poor man's enthusiasm; it is not really a word. At best, *enthused* is informal and should be avoided.

### *every day* vs *everyday*

*Every day* (two words) is an adjective noun combination meaning "each day" or "every single day."

*Everyday* (one word) is an adjective meaning "usual" or "ordinary." *Everyday* is used with a noun or pronoun.

> Every day was filled with the everyday concerns of a trapper.
>
> He sported his everyday hat every day except Sunday when he wore his Stetson.

### *every one* vs *everyone*

(See **any one** vs **anyone**.)

*Every one* (two words) is an adjective-pronoun combination indicating every single indefinite one of something. Even though "every" precedes the "one," it is a singular entity requiring a singular verb. Usually the preposition *of* or a noun follows *everyone* (one word).

*Everyone* is a pronoun synonymous with *everybody*. *Every one* is not synonymous with *everybody* and attempting to substitute *everybody* can give you an idea as to correct usage.

> Every one of us can whoop your butt, Big Jake. (You cannot say: "Everybody of us…")
>
> For every one trapper there's a thousand Indians. (You cannot say: "For everybody trapper…")

Everyone mistakes Big Jake for a mangy old bear. (Here you can say: "Everybody mistakes…")

### *everyone* vs *anyone*

Which of the following is correct?

He is the most ornery crittur of anyone I know.

He is the most ornery crittur of everyone I know.

The first sentence is incorrect. Consider the logic of what you are saying in this sentence. Can you readily conceptualize someone being the *most* ornery of *any one* individual you know?

The second sentence is correct. Everyone, though singular, is plural in the sense of how it is used. The words *most ornery* encompass a vast conceptual whole and compare one crittur to many others. In this usage, *everyone* makes more sense than *anyone*.

You could, however, correctly say: He is *more* ornery than anyone I know. Here *more* makes a comparison, one to one other.

❖❖❖❖❖

When the missionaries came west they found the mountain man more appalling than the Indian, for the Indian was just a heathen; the mountain man was white. The mountain man actually chose the life he lived. He wore animal skins and he was weathered so dark and smelled so bad you could hardly tell him from an Indian anyway. The mountain man sat on the earth and slept nestled in the blowing grass beneath the stars that twinkled above the dark treetops. He ate his food before open fires. He smoked tobacco and drank whiskey when and where he wanted, and he warred with red man, white man, and God himself when he believed he had cause. He took a squaw or two and lived with his wives among the savages in open sin. Well, the missionaries had come to change all that.

---

### *everyplace* vs *everywhere*

Grammatically speaking, one should not be seen in the following places (either in mixed company or alone): *everyplace, anyplace, someplace, no place.* All of these places are an informal abomination of American grammar and should be shunned and spurned and otherwise avoided at all cost.

Instead use: *everywhere, anywhere, somewhere, nowhere.*

Now you're getting somewhere, crittur.

### *final* vs *finalize*

*Final* is an adjective. There is the noun *finality. Finally* (adverb), there's *finalize* which is supposed to mean to put into a final form. It may be all right to use *finalize* in informal writing, but avoid the word in a formal proposal of marriage, a ransom note, a death threat, or other important correspondence.

### *flammable, inflammable, nonflammable*

*Flammable* and *inflammable* both mean capable of burning; likely to burn. *Nonflammable* means incapable of burning; not likely to burn. *Inflammable* can also indicate a situation where passion or anger is easily aroused.

### *forebears, forbear, four bears*

*Forebears* are your ancestors. *Forbear* means to refrain or hold back. *Four bears* is one more than three bears.

There's trouble when four bears are hungry, and they're looking at you as though you were wearing a "cheap-eats" sign around your neck, and one bear understands that *cheap* is an adjective and *eats* is a noun, while another bear considers *cheap* and *eats* as a single entity noun; the third bear who is only semi-literate mistakenly takes *cheap* as an adverb and *eats* as a verb, and sadly, the other bears have no interest in stopping to correct his grammar. The fourth bear can't read at all, but he intends to eat the sign right after he eats you.

### *forego* vs *forgo*

*Forego* is a transitive verb meaning to precede in time or to precede (another) to a place.

*Forgo* means to abstain from doing something; to give up something.

### *former* vs *latter*

*Former* and *latter* are comparisons and should only be used in reference to two things being compared.

The reader is confused when *former* and *latter* are used in reference to three or more things.

### generally *vs* usually

*Generally* refers to, relates to, or affects the whole. It suggests a thing is prevalent, or characteristic of most members or entities being considered. *Usually* has nothing to do with numbers as percentages of the whole. *Usually* means commonly experienced, commonly the case, customarily encountered.

There are times you may wish to use *generally* for *usually* because sometimes *generally* strikes a folksy note, or seems to hit the right nerve. Nonetheless, critturs should be aware of the differences.

### graduate *vs* graduated

*Graduate* is a verb denoting the act of conferring a college degree or high school diploma. Hence:

> I was graduated from high school. (Of course, this is the passive voice.)
>
> I graduated from high school. (This active voice is now preferable to the passive voice which in earlier years had more currency.)

Avoid *graduate* as a transitive verb when it means to receive an academic degree or diploma from. The sentence below is considered incorrect by most grammarians.

> I graduated high school.

### *have* vs *of*

Use *have*, not *of*, after *could*, *would*, and *should*. The problem here seems to have originated in the contractions *could've*, *should've*, and *would've* which sound the same as *could of*, *would of*, and *should of* to the unknowing, unthinking, easily fooled ear.

### *historic* vs *historical*

The word *historic* refers to what had or what was significant in the past, or what is happening today that is so important as to have significance in the future as history or the study of history or the study of antiquity.

> The sale of the Louisiana Territory by Napoleon was historic.

The word historical can refer to anything in the past whether or not it was of any importance to mankind in general.

> Wiley Willie becoming the first man to kiss Moose-face Maggie Marlow was an historical moment in her life. His life, too.

(See Articles and Vowel Sounds.)

### *imminent* vs *eminent*

*Imminent* is what is going to happen (usually something bad) right away or at any time soon. *Eminent* denotes importance in rank, prominence, worthiness, noteworthiness.

## *impact*

You are safe using *impact* as a noun. Things can get a little uncertain when you use *impact* as a transitive verb. You are way out on a shaky limb using *impact* as an intransitive verb. As the years go by, however, the use of *impact* as a verb of any kind is gaining currency. Shame on us for allowing our language to degrade so.

> Safe (noun): The impact of the explosion was felt for five miles.
>
> Transitive verb: The explosion impacts the confidence of the sleepy community.
>
> Intransitive verb: The explosion impacted along the houses and shops.

## *in, into, in to*

*To* is generally a preposition. *In* can be various parts of speech. Here we'll discuss *to* as a preposition. We'll discuss *in* as an adverb and as a preposition.

> Adverb: He walked in.
>
> Preposition: He walked in the room.
>
> Preposition: He walked into the room.

So, what is the difference between "He walked *in* the room" and "He walked *into* the room"? It depended on whether you are speaking or writing from an inside or outside perspective,

If you are already in the river, you can jump up and down *in* the river. You are inside the river. If someone is outside the river on the river bank and is watching you and thinks you are having fun, he may then want to jump *into* the river to join you.

If you are inside a room pacing back and forth, you are walking *in* the room. If another person enters the room through the open door, that person is walking *into* the room.

(See **on** vs **onto**.)

So, what about *in to*? When *in* is an adverb followed by an infinitive, you get the following:

> When the angry, wounded bear went into its cave, Big Jake went in to get it.
>
> When the angry, wounded bear went into (preposition) its cave, Big Jake went *in* (adverb) *to get it*. (infinitive phrase)

### *infer* vs *imply*

*Infer* connotes some information or some concept *taken in*. When one *infers*, one surmises or draws a conclusion from what is written, spoken, or presented by someone else or something else.

*Imply* connotes some information or some concept *given out*. When one *implies*, one suggests or conveys a meaning without actually stating it.

> He called me a drunkard and a scoundrel unfit to marry his daughter. His harsh words, the inflection in his voice, the double-barreled shotgun in his one hand, the rope in his other hand, and the armed posse standing behind him

*implied* a tough night lay ahead for me. I *inferred* from his demeanor that my drinking, brawling, carousing, gambling, cheating, and horse stealing had not stood me in good stead with my future father-in-law. The fact that I hung out with Big Jake didn't help either.

### intense *vs* intent

*Intense* means profound (intense pain), something done to an extreme degree, exerting a supreme effort.

*Intent* means determined (intent on murder), something intended, a purpose, an aim, end, or a goal; firmly fixed in the mind, engrossed.

*Intent* suggests deliberateness stronger than mere intention.

His intention was to gather as many pelts as he could before the summer warmth ended the season.

He was intent on passing through Blackfoot territory and coming out alive.

*Goal* connotes an idealistic or remote purpose.

*End* suggests a long range goal.

*Aim* stresses the direction of one's efforts in pursuit of an end.

*Object* is an end one tries to achieve.

*Objective* implies the end or goal is, indeed, attainable.

### *irregardless*, *regardless*, *irrespective*

*Irregardless* is not a word and is banned in all territories west of the Mississippi. However, it is sometimes acceptable in remote outposts late at night when the whiskey is flowing freely.

The problem is, once you add the negative *less* as a suffix to the base word, the negative prefix *ir* is redundant. Use *regardless* instead. If you still like the emphasis of the *ir*, use *irrespective*; it means *without regard to*.

### *learn* *vs* *teach*

*Learn* means to acquire knowledge. *Teach* means to impart knowledge, to help another learn.

> Incorrect: "I'll learn ya, boy, ifin' it's the larst thing I does."

### *led* *vs* *lead*

As a noun, *lead* is a base metal. *Lead* is dull-gray and heavy.

*Lead* is a verb meaning to guide, to go before, and show the way.

*Led* is the past tense of the verb lead.

### *lend, loan, borrow*

*Lend* is a verb meaning to give or grant the temporary use of something. (Money is usually lent at interest.)

*Borrow* means to receive something (or money) lent to you for a period of time.

*Loan* is a noun meaning the actual thing (or money) given or lent for temporary use.

> Incorrect: "Will you loan me twenty dollars?" asked Parker Daniels.
> Correct: "Will you lend me twenty dollars?" asked Parker Daniels.
> "No way, Parker Daniels! You never paid me back the last loan."

*The American Heritage High School Dictionary* may disagree with me here, noting that in America, loan is well established as a verb referring only to tangible transactions such as money or goods. Accordingly, the *American Heritage* folks would agree that the following sentence still requires lend because that which is lent is intangible:

**"Time lends a mellowness to old memories and old socks."**

🖘 **Stinky Petey**

And, critturs everywhere, the word is moneylender. Even we rowdy Americans would never say, "Shylock was a moneyloaner."

### *less* vs *few*

Do not use *less* when you mean *few*. *Few* denotes individual items or people you can number or count. *Less* refers to the overall bulk, an unspecified quantity of something.

Incorrect: We have less trappers out today than we had yesterday.

Correct: We have fewer trappers out today than we had yesterday.

Incorrect: Henry Wells lived in St. Louis less than four years.

Correct: Henry Wells lived in St. Louis fewer than four years.

He would have been better off with fewer wives and less whiskey.

Fewer than five showed up to help.

We had less than twenty pounds of flour. (an overall bulk; an amount)

We had fewer than twenty sacks of flour. (The sacks are countable, individual items.)

Many young men ventured westward. Few gained the legendary status of Jim Bridger and Kit Carson.

### *libel* vs *slander*

*Libel* denotes a defamation by means of published material in print, photographs, drawings, graphics, writing, or in any manner other than the spoken word or gestures. *Libel* injures a person. The mere intent to injure is enough to determine libel. If intent to injure can be proven, a writer and/or his publisher may be guilty of libel—even if what was written or depicted was true, and even if the injured person is a public figure.

*Slander* is also defamation, but slander is defamation by means of the spoken word, or by gestures if one is creative enough and possesses the adequate deftness of fingers, hands, and arms to get his point across. Again, one may be found guilty of slander if it can be proven that the intent was to injure. The lesson here is that everyone should "play nice" at all times. (See **likely, liable, libel**.)

### *lie, lay, lain*
Generally (there are exceptions), the verb *lie* is an intransitive verb and does not take a direct object. *Lay* is transitive and takes a direct object—except when *lay* is the past tense of *lie*.

*Lie* means to rest or recline; recumbent. *Lay* means to put down, place down, prepare, or put in place. *Lie* also means a falsehood and to prevaricate or dissemble.

| Present Tense | Present Participle | Past Tense | Past participle |
|---|---|---|---|
| lie | lying | lay | have/had lain |
| lay | laying | laid | have/had laid |

The verb *lie* is an intransitive verb and does not take an object.

> She often *lies* down after dinner.
> I was *lying* in my bedroll when he hollered out.

When *lay* is the past tense of the intransitive verb *lie*, *lay* is also intransitive. First determine whether your sentence has a direct object. From there you can decide whether of not to use *lie* (intransitive), *lay* (intransitive), or *lay* (transitive).

> Yesterday, I lay down to sleep. (*Lay* is the past tense of *lie* and is intransitive.)
>
> When I lay down, I fell asleep. (Here again *lay* is the past tense of *lie*. *Down* is an adverb here; there is no direct object.)
>
> I'm so tired I could lie down to sleep in cactus briars. (intransitive)
>
> He had lain in cactus briars all day. (intransitive)
>
> History lies in legend. (intransitive)

When the verb *lay* is transitive, it needs a direct object.

> Lay that pistol down, woman! (The direct object is *pistol*.)
>
> He was laying his traps. (The direct object is *traps*.)
>
> He laid his anger at the threshold and stepped inside. (The direct object is *anger*.)

The reason why some readers have never even heard of the verb *lain* is because those readers have not read the classics, and/or because skillful writers have learned early on how to circumvent the word.

Instead of writing: The wounded soldiers
had lain there a week.

A skillful writer writes: The wounded soldiers lay there a week.

The wounded bear lay in ambush.

When to use *lain* and when to use *laid* depends again on whether the sentence has a direct object.

He has lain asleep all day. (intransitive—no direct object)

He has laid a heavy burden upon himself. (transitive—the direct object is *burden*)

### *likely, liable, libel*

*Likely* means probable, plausible, or appropriate. *Likely* is more properly used as an adverb or adjective. As an adverb, *likely* is usually preceded by "quite," "very," or another qualifier.

He will very likely haunt my dreams for the rest of my life. (adverb)

He is a likely suspect. (adjective)

He is likely to find beaver dams upstream. (adjective)

Using the adverb *likely* without a qualifier is generally acceptable, but don't push it in formal writing.

Pushing it: He'll likely get himself killed if
he goes wandering into Ute country.

*Liable* means legally responsible.

By writing a letter of introduction for
Sagebrush Sam, Stinky Petey became
liable for litigation when, over a three-
month period of time, Sagebrush Sam
swindled the Hubert and Goober Bank
out of thirty thousand dollars. In his
defense, Sagebrush Sam said it was an
accident.

*Libel*: If you are guilty of libel, you have published a false and/or malicious report intended to
damage the reputation of another person. You
can—and probably will—get yourself entangled in
a very messy, very expensive lawsuit for the
attempt to injure, or the actual injury of someone
with words as your weapon of choice. (See **libel** vs
**slander**.)

## may be *vs* maybe
*May* is used to express a wish, contingency, possibility, or permission.

May it ever be so. (wish)
Our hope is that he may be safe.
    (contingency)
I may be silly, but… (possibility)

It may be snowing in the mountains.
  (possibility)
You may go now. (permission)

*Maybe* means perhaps. Perhaps something may happen. Perhaps something is possible.

Maybe I'm silly, but…
Maybe it's snowing in the mountains.
Maybe you should go now.

### meanwhile, in the meanwhile, meantime

Do not say, "In the meanwhile, I went home" because *meanwhile* is an adverb and *in* is a preposition. The object of a preposition needs to be either a noun or pronoun—never an adverb. Simply say, "Meanwhile, I went home" or "In the meantime, I went home." Here *meantime* is a noun and serves quite well as the object of the preposition *in*.

### meddle, metal, mettle

The noun *metal* is—well, the hard stuff—the minerals in the earth you can heat and mold and forge and hammer and buff and shine and give names to like gold, silver, copper, etc.

The noun *mettle* is courage, pluck, gumption, and rugged determination.

The verb *meddle* is something nosey, snoopy folks do in the eastern cities. Out west, a crittur usually meddles only once, as west of St. Louis, meddling can have deadly consequences.

### *no body* vs *nobody*

*Nobody* is a pronoun. *No* can be an adverb, adjective, even a noun.

> Nobody liked her. She was troublesome—a skinny girl with no body.

### *noisome* vs *noisy*

*Noisy* means a lot of noise; loud, shrill, disturbing sound.

*Noisome* means offensive, disgusting, nauseous, even harmful or injurious to health.

### *on* vs *onto*

*On* indicates an inside perspective; *onto* indicates an outside perspective. (See **in, into, in to**.) When you use *on* as an adverb, do not attach it to the preposition *to*.

> The discussion moved on to (not *onto*) new concerns.
>
> He walked on the grass. (This sentence means he was already on the grass when he started walking.)
>
> He walked onto the grass. (This sentence means he was not on the grass initially, but then he walked, maybe from the rock ledge, onto the grass.)

### *on, upon, up on*

*On* and *upon* can sometimes be interchangeable. Both of the below sentences are correct:

The frost lay on the ground.
The frost lay upon the ground.

But *on* and *upon* are not always interchangeable.

I'll buy the saddle on (not *upon*) that horse.
He spoke on (not *upon*) the subject of treaties.

When *up* is an adverb and *on* is a preposition, do not join them as one word.

He was quite a trapper up on the Yellowstone.

---

Big Jake McLaughlin knew death comes soon enough to all men, and he was kind of just resting up for it, getting by each day with no intention of outdoing anyone or cheating anyone out of anything. He enjoyed the cool mornings and the smell of coffee steaming over a campfire. He ate when he was hungry, slept when he was tired, and made love to his woman when the urge was upon him. His days were spent wandering the sunlight and shadows of the high woods, the dappled, the dark, and the dank. There he walked with God in the free, wild earthy essence, there with the ever-pervasive scent of the fallen leaves carried on the wind. There in the high forests were the scented flowering plants; there were the beaver and the game animals and maybe a fleeting sighting of the fox.

These were the things that made his heart beat inside his chest.

———◆▸◗◖◂◆———

### *or* *vs* *nor*

Do not use the conjunction *nor* after a negative unless the conjunction joins a compound sentence. A compound sentence consists of two independent clauses joined by a comma and a conjunction, or a semicolon.

> Incorrect: Calls Down the Stars does not cheat nor steal.
>
> Correct: Calls Down the Stars does not cheat or steal.
>
> Correct: She will not nag or argue.
>
> Correct: She will not cuss, nor will she drink whiskey. (This is correct because a comma and the conjunction nor join the compound sentence.)

But, remember that *neither* and *nor* complement each other, and *nor* should follow *neither* as in: "Neither rain, nor snow, nor sleet..."

"...neither noble, nor brave..."

> Correct: Stinky Petey had an aversion to water, especially if soap was introduced into the equation. He could neither float nor swim. He would not bathe or change his clothes. (He would neither bathe nor change his clothes.)

Use *nor* when the negative in the first part of a compound sentence continues to be expressed in the second part of the compound sentence, and the subject and object in the first part invert in the second part.

> Big Jake never trusted Sagebrush Sam, nor did Sagebrush Sam ever trust Big Jake.

But if the second part of the compound sentence is simply a verbal phrase and not an independent clause, you may drop the *nor* and use *or*. Both of the following sentences are correct. The first sentence is preferred by old-timers like me and Strunk and White.

> Big Jake did not like Sagebrush Sam, or trust him.
> Big Jake did not like Sagebrush Sam, nor trust him.

You are safe recasting your sentence in one of the following ways:

> Big Jake neither liked Sagebrush Sam, nor trusted him.
> Big Jake neither liked Sagebrush Sam, nor did he trust him.
> Big Jake did not like or trust Sagebrush Sam.

*Or* is more widely used when a noun phrase, adjective phrase, or adverb phrase follows the verb.

When *no* or *not* precedes or begins a noun phrase, usually *no*, rather than *not* is used to continue the following element of the sentence:

> Parker Daniels had a run of bad luck. He had no money or means. He was not smart or lucky.

### passed *vs* past

The word *passed* is always a verb. *Passed* is the past tense of the verb *pass*. *Pass* means to move, to move past, to go beyond, to complete (a test) successfully. *Past* is an adjective meaning earlier or former, a noun meaning the time gone by, the history of something, an adverb meaning so as to pass by, a preposition meaning beyond in space, time, number, or amount.

> He was *past* his prime. (preposition)
> He walked *past* the cabin. (preposition)
> He *passed* his prime. (verb)
> She *passed* the test. (verb)
> The quick wolf ran *past* and *passed* the slow dog, which was also running *past*. (adverb, verb, and adverb)
> In the *past* I *passed* this very creek and never stopped to pan for gold. (noun and verb)

### passerby *vs* passers-by

A *passerby* is a person who walks by, or somehow passes by something else, hence, a *passerby*. The proper plural is *passersby* or *passers-by*—indicting more than one person passing by.

### pedal *vs* peddle

As a noun, *pedal* is a lever you operate with your foot. As a verb, it's the act of propelling yourself (on a bicycle, etc.) by working the pedals.

Peddle means to carry around items for the purpose of selling them. A traveling salesman peddles his wares.

### penal *vs* penile

A women's prison is *penal*, not *penile*. Just wanted to clear that up, crittur.

### people *vs* persons

*People* usually connotes vast numbers; *persons* usually connotes smaller groups where the number can be counted.

> The people who ventured west were mostly adventurers, runaways, and businessmen.
> Three persons were killed in an Indian raid.

Use *persons* sparingly so your sentences do not sound stilted and pompous. Try to use exact nouns whenever possible. Instead of writing "Three persons were killed in an Indian raid," write:

> Three *trappers* were killed in an Indian raid.

**or**

Three *settlers* escaped from a Cheyenne war party as soldiers from the 7th Cavalry...

### *per* vs *according to*

Only use *per* in those out of the way dives where people with whom you would never want to hang out are showing off their Latin.

> "*Per se*, Buffy, precious, what *percent* of the *per capita* in this wilderness is employed on a *per diem* basis, eh?"
> "Employed, Dudley—as in *working*?"
> "Yes, pet."
> "I believe, Dudley, darling, the tally is over a third *percent, per* the fur company records."
> "How dreadful, Buffy!"

Actually, using *percent* is all right to express the legitimate relationship of a two digit number to the number one hundred. Buffy, however, mixed her fractions with her percents. Instead of saying "a third percent," she should have said "thirty-three and a third percent." But that's Buffy, and she'll never change.

*Per* is acceptable in business (twenty dollars per person), or for calculating (sixty miles per hour, thirty miles per gallon).

But, as per most grammarians, a writer or speaker should avoid *per*. Whenever possible, use *according to* instead of *per* so as not to sound, well, *per contra*.

> Avoid: He arrived at dawn, as per instructions.
>
> Better: He arrived at dawn, according to instructions.

**pore, pour** *(And We'll Throw in **poor**—No Charge)*

*Poor* means: Impoverished, indigent, lacking value.

*Pore* means to read over, to ponder, study, examine, peruse carefully.

*Pore* also means a tiny opening in the skin or a space in a rock or soil.

*Pour* means to cause a liquid or granular solid to flow as from a bottle, pitcher, or other container.

———◆◆◆◆———

Jim Bridger was a *poor* boy apprenticed to a blacksmith in the river town of St. Louis. For five long years the lad toiled before the forge and honorably lived out his contract. As the grime blackened his arms and the sweat glistened from his *pores*, Jim Bridger dreamed westward to the freedom and adventure of the mountains.

As soon as his apprenticeship was completed, young Jim Bridger was keen to go. On March 20, 1822, the Missouri Republican carried a notice calling for a hundred young men to sign on with Major Andrew Henry for an ascent up the Missouri River for a "one, two, or three year" adventure, or so Jim had heard. Being illiterate, Jim Bridger could not read the notice himself.

Bridger brought the newspaper to his best friend Big Jake McLaughlin who could read some. The big guy spread the newspaper on the table before him and *poured* himself a cup of coffee. Jim Bridger looked on in wonder and admiration at a man who could read words. Big Jake *pored* through the advertisements and notices until he came to Major Henry's call for men.

"You're right, Hoss," Big Jake said, "this is something we might just be interested in." On those heady heights of exhilaration, Jim Bridger did not care that his friend Big Jake McLaughlin had committed a grammatical faux pas by ending his sentence with a preposition.

---

### *precipitate* vs *precipitous*

Besides its meteorological implications, *precipitate* means to cause to occur suddenly or prematurely, or to move quickly and recklessly.

*Precipitous* means of or resembling a precipice. *Precipitous* should not be used to indicate haste, heedless, headlong speed, or the absence of due deliberation. To use *precipitous* to mean hasty or abrupt is outright wrong.

> We camped in the high spruce where the mountainside sloped precipitously to the dark valley below. That night a band of Ute warriors swept into camp precipitately and killed three of our company.

### predicament *vs* dilemma

*Predicament* refers to trouble—big trouble—as Georgie Custer had trouble at the Little Big Horn River. *Dilemma* indicates there is a troublesome choice that must be made. Since the seven or so thousand Indians at the Little Big Horn did not leave open many avenues of choice for Georgie and his crew of a couple of hundred brave troopers, one may refer to that time and that place as Custer's predicament, not Custer's dilemma. Disaster, catastrophe, fiasco, and debacle also come to mind.

### principal *vs* principle

*Principal* means of the highest importance. A *principal* is the director or chief administrator of a school. A *principal* is a person who engages an agent or another to represent him. *Principal* also refers to an amount of capital (money) other than, separate from, or otherwise distinguished from interest, profit, or subsequent capital gain of any kind.

The word *principle* denotes a generally accepted or elemental truth, a fundamental law of nature or man, a basic rule or reality as a premise for a polemic. *Principle* also means a rule of moral, ethical, honorable conduct. A principled person—a highly principled person—conducts himself with honor, chivalry, civility, and dignity.

For young student critturs: When you refer to the principal of your school, remember that the princi*pal* is your pal; spell it accordingly.

Big Jake saw no value in wasted emotion. There was no sense in wishing things could have been different. His happiness was the woods and the wind, the roaring rivers, the fast, cold streams, and the clear mountain lakes. He loved the simple things. There was the haunting glow of foxfire in the dark of night. And in the wash of creek beds were the water-smooth little stones that glistened in the cool morning sunlight.

In his wanderings he would carry with him a few pieces of foxfire and a smooth "lucky rock" or two from a creek bed. These things made him happy. Here in the mountains were the easy gliding eagle and the high circling hawk; in the gathering darkness came the haunting call of the loon, the cry of the whippoorwill, the hoot of the owl, and the howl of the lonely wolf. In such simplicity, and with Calls Down the Stars to warm his nights, Big Jake McLaughlin found all the happiness he could ever wish for.

### querulous vs query

*Querulous* means peevish, irritable, fretful, full of complaints. A *query* is an inquiry, usually in the form of a letter, or a question in general. A query letter on an unresolved issue can be querulous in nature.

### raise vs rise

Among its various definitions, *raise* means to lift or cause to move to a higher level or higher position.

You raise the stakes, you raise the bar, you raise your hand in greeting.

To *rise* is to stand up or get up from a supine, prone, sitting, or otherwise reclined position. You rise out of bed in the morning. The sun also rises.

### rapine, rapacious, rapturous

*Rapine* is the forcible taking of property (not your own).

*Rapacious* means given to plundering, seizing; greedy, predatory.

*Rapturous* is when you enjoy any of the above or anything that carries you away with deep emotion, joy, or love.

### ravage, ravening, ravish, ravishing

*Ravage* means to cause violent devastation and destruction (as an invading army would); to affect in such a manner.

*Ravening* means avariciously, hungrily in pursuit of prey.

*Ravish* means to rape (a woman).

*Ravishing* means sensuously attractive, enchantingly beautiful and pleasing.

It's best to not get any of these confused, crittur.

### repository *vs* depository

*Depository* is a place (usually a bank vault) where things (usually of value) are kept for safekeeping.

*Repository* is a general unspecified location where mostly abstract things are stored. The human heart is the repository of love—or some such silliness.

### reveille, revelry, reverie

*Reveille* is a rousing tune of bugle notes awakening sleeping soldiers in the morning. Soldiers hate it. *Revelry* denotes noisy, boisterous merrymaking. Soldiers love revelry. *Reverie* is daydreaming or abstracted contemplation.

> At morning *reveille*, in bittersweet *reverie*
> of the night's *revelry*, a soldier groans
> and nurses his hangover.

### sanction *vs* sanctions

If something is legally *sanctioned*, it is all right to do; it is backed by statute and the courts. If engaging in a certain activity has *sanctions* imposed against it, the activity is being punished and penalized because it is illegal or at least not appreciated by a governing power imposing or enacting such sanctions. I guess it all makes sense if you say it fast enough.

### sects *vs* sex *(hoboy!)*

A *sect* is a usually tight-knit group of individuals united by a mutually embraced doctrine. *Sex* is sex. Enough said, crittur.

### send-off *vs* send off

The noun *send-off* or *sendoff* is an outward show of good will or celebration as a person leaves for new (far off) destinations or new ventures. A person may get a joyous send-off.

The verb *send off* indicates someone or something is being sent away—dispatched, or dismissed, either under favorable, affable, or hostile circumstances. A person may decide he will send off a letter.

### set *vs* sit
Generally (there are exceptions), *set* is a transitive verb; *sit* is an intransitive verb.

> He set the trap with a hair trigger.
> (Transitive: The direct object is *trap*.)
> He would sit on the hillside and meditate.
> (Intransitive: There is no direct object.)

### setup, set up, set up
As a noun, a *setup* is something deliberately organized in advance to be easy or attainable; or a situation preplanned in such a way as to fool or deceive another.

> An ambush is a setup.

As a verb *set up* means to organize or arrange something properly.

> They set up an ambush.

*Set up* can also be an adjective meaning arranged beforehand.

> It was a set up deal.

———————◆◆◆◆◆———————

In his night camps, Big Jake was a primitive man again, sitting silhouetted at his fire. He would sit with the wind at his back, watching the fire and the wavy dance of heat, listening to the pop and the crackle of the burning wood, the roar of the flames, and he'd watch as the smoke and sparks rode the night winds to the sky. Above him the shooting stars crossed the heavens. The things he did not know could not be known, and he was content with that. The endless stars in the endless heavens were no different from the earthly treasures most men seek and never find or never hold very long. It was the things beyond a man's grasp that made his living and his dying that much dearer.

———————◆◆◆◆◆———————

### *suffering* vs *suffrage*

*Suffering* means to undergo pain, or to tolerate, permit, endure. *Suffrage* is the right to vote in a political election.

Jesus said to suffer (tolerate) the little children. He meant the little guys. He had nothing nice to say about teenagers. You've heard the expression: "He suffers fools badly." Here, again, *suffers* here means tolerates.

> Until he married Iron Skillet, Big Jake did not believe in women's suffrage.

### than *vs* then

*Than* introduces the following element of a comparison. *Than* could mean except or except for; *than* could denote something rejected.

> Other than a broken nose and missing teeth, he was fine.
>
> I'd rather kiss my donkey than kiss Moose-face Maggie Marlow.

*Then* means therefore, consequently, next, following that, or following in order.

> I kissed Moose-face Maggie. Then I sobered up.

---

The mountain man was tolerated by the Indian because the mountain man did not want the land. The mountain man just wanted to trap and hunt and wander. Other men came later for the land, men who wanted the Indian Christianized or dead, or both. These men built wooden structures; forts and settlements became towns. There were prairie towns and mountain towns and river towns and port towns, and the railroad came through and the barbed wired fences crossed the land where the buffalo once roamed free. The buffalo were gone then, and a way of life ended for the red man.

The Indian never understood it, then or now, and the right or wrong of it doesn't mean anything anymore. Americans will never again know the old wild days of the mountain man and the savage Indian. Gone, too, are the buffalo hunters, the keel boat men, and the early cowboys. The old die out and get plowed into the earth by the new. That's the sad normal nature of things. For the short years of his life, a man holds to the things he loves before it's his turn to yield to time.

---

### *to, too, two*

The word *to* is a preposition. ...go to work. ...to that end.

> He came to camp that morning.

The word *too* is an adverb meaning *also*. When *too* means *also*, you need to set it off with commas. (You do not need commas to set off the word *also* unless *also* begins a sentence as an introductory word.)

> John went, too.
> John, too, went.

The word *too* is an adverb meaning to an unusual extent or excessive degree. When *too* does not mean *also*—when it is an adverb meaning *to an excessive degree*, do not set it off with commas.

> He is too stupid to survive in the wild.
> He is too sneaky to be trusted.
> He was too fearless for his own good.

When using *too*, be sure to complete your thought.

> Incomplete: The Cheyenne scouts crept silently nearer the Crow encampment. At the edge of the first teepee, Gray Wolf assessed the situation and motioned the others to stop. It was too dangerous. (Too dangerous for what?)
>
> Complete: The Cheyenne scouts crept silently nearer the Crow encampment. At the edge of the first teepee, Gray Wolf assessed the situation and motioned the others to stop. It was too dangerous to go any closer.

The word *two* is the written numeral that comes between *one* and *three*. In case you need a more definitive definition: Most people have (or should have): *two* hands, *two* feet, *two* eyes, *two* ears, and at least *two* teeth. A man, if he's smart, has but *one* wife and speaks with *one* tongue.

Look at the next sentence. The infinitive is *to go*. Here *to* is the sign of the infinitive, not a preposition. *To* precedes the verb *go*. A preposition needs to precede its object noun or pronoun. *To go* is an infinitive serving as a noun. The last prepositional phrase is *to town*.

(See Prepositions. See Infinitives.)

> One of the two men was too drunk to go to town.

### *toward* vs *towards*

Only the Brits favor using *towards*. Don't you forget the Revolutionary War and the War of 1812, among some other skirmishes we had with them redcoats. The proper American word is *toward*.

### *want* vs *wont*

*Want* is a desire, or to be in need of something. *Wont* is another matter.

As an adjective, *wont* means in the habit of.

> She was wont to load her shotgun with rock salt and fire off both barrels at her man coming home drunk, or for his not coming home the night before when he was drunk, for his gambling and straying, and for various and sundry minor indiscretions to which a man was partial and otherwise predisposed.
> Stinky Petey was wont to offend any living creature down wind of him.

*Wonted* means customary by force of habit.

> He enjoyed his wonted evening smoke by the fireside.

As a noun, *wont* means a customary condition or practice, one's usual behavior.

> It was his wont to shoot first and ask questions only while he was reloading. (paraphrasing Saul DeVitt)

As a verb *wont* is kind of, sort of archaic. It means to accustom.

> Wont your morals to probity. (Hey, I warned
> you it was mostly archaic.)

### *where, when, that*

*Where* should not be used in place of *when* or *that*.

> Rendezvous is a summertime celebration
> *when* (not *where*) the trappers gather
> together for fun, folly, drinking, gam-
> bling, trading, and serious socializing.
> On a wanted poster, I read *that* (not *where*)
> Big Jake was popular with the marshal
> in St. Louis.

### *who vs whom*

Some modern grammarians are calling for the aboli-
tion of *whom*. They claim *whom* is rarely used today,
and when it is used, it is confusing and mostly used
incorrectly. Those grammarians are idiots. Pay them
no heed, crittur. The use of *who* and *whom* is really
quite simple.

Who is a subject pronoun; *whom* is an object pronoun. *Who* does the action; *whom* receives the
action.

> Who gave what to whom? (*Who* is the sub-
> ject. *Whom* is the object of the preposi-
> tion *to*.)

*Whom* is always the object of the verb or the object of the preposition. If your sentence has a preposition you are always safe in using *whom* as its object.

> To whom is she speaking? (*She* is the subject sandwiched between the split verb *is speaking*; *whom* is the object of the preposition *to*.)
>
> Whom would you ask to go with you? (The verb is *would ask*. The verb is split and the subject *you* is sandwiched in between. *You would ask whom to go with you? Whom* is the direct object.)

With these guidelines in mind, use *whom* freely and fearlessly.

———◆◆◆◆———

No one ever knew how it ended for Big Jake McLaughlin. One morning in late autumn, when the breeze was rising gentle and crisp along the mountainside, when the smell of the earth and fallen leaves was in the air, when the morning sun came slanting through the trees in needle points that hurt his eyes, Big Jake gathered his possibles and saddled his horse.

Outside their cabin, he held Calls Down the Stars close and tight and kissed her long and hard. Then he gave her a playful slap on her rump—a little too hard she thought, but she smiled up at him in spite of herself. Calls Down the Stars was with child, but it was early and she wasn't showing and she hadn't told Big Jake. He would be back when the rivers froze solid, and she would tell him then.

Big Jake mounted his horse and she waved as he rode away, the big horse making its way up through the dark trees and shadows of the mountainside. Big Jake did not return the wave, but he looked back at the woman and gave her that wonderful smile she loved, that flash of white teeth, and he rode off to the mountains, through the shadows, and disappeared into the trees.

Calls Down the Stars waited all through that winter and into the spring, but Big Jake did not return. In late spring she had her baby. The baby was a girl and she called her Jake and the world could go to hell if they didn't like the name. The summer came and was gone and the autumn winds began to blow. Big Jake had not returned, and people would say whatever they would say, but Calls Down the Stars knew. Somewhere in the high mountains Big Jake McLaughlin had made his final trade. The woman held the baby to her breast as she looked toward the far mountains and the high forest. Her man would not be coming home, and no matter how it had happened or when, Big Jake would have considered it a fair enough trade.

Congratulations, crittur! We've blazed a long trail together. We may part ways for a little while, but from now on, your stick floats with mine. I hereby confer upon you the titles of:

※ **MASTER OF THE SENTENCE,
KEEPER OF THE DOGS AND PONIES,
LORD OF THE FLOAT STICK,
USUFRUCTUARY OF USAGE, PROTECTOR
OF THE PRONOUN, VIRTUOSO OF VERBS,
MINISTER OF MODIFIERS, SAVIOR OF
THE VERBALS, CONQUEROR OF THE
CONJUNCTION, DEFENDER OF CLAUSES,
GUARDIAN OF PHRASES, ORACLE OF
ORTHOGRAPHY, SAVANT OF STYLE,
FANCY OF DANCY, AND FELICITATOR
OF FOOFARAW** ※

# Epilogue

---

The mountain man and the old wild America are gone. Still, Americans continue to dream big.

America is as much a concept as it is a nation, unique in all the world. As the years press onward and as long as we continue to understand that America is God's gift to men of courage and vision, this great land will continue its grandeur. America will ever be new and exciting, finding its own dreams, facing its own challenges, and renewing its old glory. In courage, honor, generosity, and brotherhood, men and women of all colors, creeds, and nationalities will keep on being stubbornly, audaciously, uniquely American. And America will continue to be God's good land of promise and adventure.

# Glossary

Under pressure from prevailing forces—mostly on the distaff end of the balance scale—the author has assembled this brief glossary of terms used in this book. He was especially asked to clarify *loath, loathe,* and *loathsome.* Generally, most other terms in this book have been explained within the pages and text. I think.

**cohort:** An associate or companion. In modern usage the word has a connotation of nefariousness, or at best, a vague quality or concept of "ne'er-do-well" attending the relationship of companions, those "known to hang out with," and others "seen in the company of."

**coup:** A successful strike. In Indian terms a coup was an act of supreme courage—derring-do, if you will, not necessarily resulting in the death of an enemy, more the total disregard of danger, as in the thick of battle a warrior rode up or ran up close enough to touch or strike an enemy. Killing the enemy was not actually looked down upon, it was simply not necessary.

I suppose it was more humiliating to just walk up and smack your enemy a good shot across his knobby head.

**draw:** A low drainage area of land where water accumulates or drains from a river, creek, etc. An unwary crittur—one who does not yet know the way the stick floats—may, in times of drought, not readily recognize a draw. A savvy mountain man, however, can always tell a draw by the lay of the land, by the ground patterns, by the plant life, and by the shape of the rocks and how they lay upon the surface. Even in times of drought, it is usually not a good idea to set up camp in a draw. If you doubt that, just ask Drowned-Rat Eddie Briscoll.

**flint:** A hard stone of silica which, when struck against steel, will (if everything goes right) produce a spark that can be gently blown in and through dry tinder, and coaxed into a roaring fire. This process works extremely well when it works well, though as the author can attest, it is less reliable than the standard fire drill or the old hand drill.

**grammarian:** A term for a self-serving, self-centered, pedantic, bombastic, pseudo-intelligent ninny who can tell you, quite nasally, how to conjugate a verb, but doesn't have enough sense to know when he's crossing a cow pasture at night and his hat blows off to just let it go rather than attempt to stumble about in the dark picking things up and putting them on his head.

**grippe:** An old-fashioned term for a heavy cold or influenza.

**grifter:** A swindler or confidence man. The term applies to such characters as Parker Daniels and Zeke Hatcher, and to a lesser extent Soft-Headed Sylvester who was just a horse thief, and Stinky Petey who wasn't much of anything but couldn't exactly be trusted. It was Stinky Petey's saving grace that he never really succeeded at anything he ever attempted.

**hobble:** The tying of a horses front legs with a loose length of rope or strap from leg to leg, so that the horse may maneuver about to graze while not able to run or stray very far away—at least in theory. In reality, hobbled horses have been known to wander for miles. A note of caution: It is generally not a good idea to attempt to hobble a horse by its hind legs.

**hogshead:** A wooden barrel with its staves held tightly in place with hoops or bands of steel. Whereas modern barrels usually hold 55 gallons, hogsheads hold from 63 to 140 gallons. Used as a term of liquid measure, hogshead is equivalent to 63 gallons. That's a lot of whiskey for a mountain man.

**Indian:** An accepted term for the red man of the Americas. The term Native American is currently experiencing some controversy because of mounting, though obviously hotly disputed evidence that the Indian was not the first human inhabitant of North or South America.

**loath:** Averse, disinclined, reluctant, or unwilling.

**loathe:** A feeling of intense disgust or absolute hatred for someone or something.

**loathsome:** Causing or exciting intense disgust or absolute hatred.

**medicine:** Magic; spiritual magic or protection (good medicine) bestowed by the spirit-gods.

**parts of speech:** The elements that in proper speech and writing make up a complete sentence, identified in words labeled as *nouns, pronouns, verbs, adjectives, adverbs, conjunctions, prepositions,* or *interjections.* In less than proper speech and writing these same eight labels may still be used to designate stray, errant words and phrases.

**pemmican:** Dried or shredded (usually buffalo) meat mixed with fat and/or berries and used as a food source.

**proper grammar and usage:** A somewhat interpretive term referring to the oral or written ordering of words, generally believed to be done on purpose, so as to effect a manner of communication widely accepted as correct in its adherence to stilted, grandiloquent, sometimes ostentatious application.

**shaman:** An Indian medicine man or holy man; a man gifted by the spirit-gods to perform spiritual healings or to see visions foretelling the future.

**squaw:** A now derogatory term for an Indian woman, especially a wife. The term is used only, and acceptable only, in historical context. Sometimes, though, if you know the gal really well and you are mutually amorously disposed toward each other, and maybe "keeping company," or maybe married to her, and she lets you call her that, and she doesn't mind or she doesn't kill you for saying it, you are mostly all right in using the term. Generally, however, Indian women are too precious, too noble, too beautiful, too gentle of spirit to ever use that term in direct address.

# BIBLIOGRAPHY

How does one write a grammar reference to top Jan Venolia's *Write Right!*, Patricia T. O'Conner's *Woe is I*, Margaret Shertzer's *The Elements of Grammar*, or Strunk and White's *The Elements of Style*? How does one rewrite the great comprehensive textbooks from MacMillan/McGraw-Hill, McDougal Littell, or John E. Warriner of Harcourt Brace Jovanovich? How does any one person define it clearer or present it plainer than the panel of usage experts of Houghton Mifflin's *The American Heritage High School Dictionary*? They, and others, are among the originals and the best. I hope, looking down from heaven or up from hell—they are at least amused at my attempt.

These grammar and style resources are some of the best available. I could not write effectively without them. The other books mentioned here on mountain men, Indians, horses, and trapping have been old friends on long winter nights.

- *The American Heritage High School Dictionary*, 3rd ed., Boston: Houghton Mifflin Company, 2000.
- *The United Press International (UPI) Stylebook*, 3rd ed., Lincolnwood, IL: National Textbook Company, 1992.
- *Webster's Unabridged Dictionary of the English Language*, based on the 2nd Edition of *The Random House Dictionary of the English Language*, New York: Random House, 2001.

- Flexner, Stuart Berg and Stein, Jess, *The Random House Dictionary* (paperback), New York: Random House, 1980.
- O'Conner, Patricia T., *Woe is I*, New York: G.P. Putnam's Sons, 1996.
- Shertzer, Margaret, *The Elements of Grammar*, New York: MacMillan Publishing, 1986.
- Stein, Jess, *The Random House Dictionary of the English Language (Unabridged)*, New York: Random House, 1967.
- Strunk, William, Jr. and E.B. White, *The Elements of Style*, 3rd ed., New York: MacMillan Publishing, 1979.
- Venolia, Jan, *Write Right!*, 3rd ed., Berkeley, CA: Ten Speed Press, 1995.

Then there are all the school textbooks from which I've taught:

- *Language Arts Today* (series), New York: MacMillan/McGraw-Hill, 1991.
- *The Writer's Craft* (series), Boston: The McDougal Littell (a Houghton Mifflin Company), 1998.
- Kemper, Dave, Meyer, Verne, Sebranek, Patrick, *Writers Inc*, Boston: Write Source (a Houghton Mifflin Company), 1996.
- Kemper, Dave, Meyer, Verne, Sebranek, Patrick, *Write Source 2000*, Boston: Write Source (a Houghton Mifflin Company), 1995.
- Warriner, John E., *Warriner's English Grammar and Composition (Second Course)*, Orlando: Harcourt Brace Jananovich, 1986.

In the course of teaching over the years, I've occasionally stumbled across books for very young readers. But a good source is a good source, and even as an adult I've learned intriguing things from such books. I have found the following books interesting, indeed:

* Anderson, C.W., C.W. *Anderson's Complete Book of Horses and Horsemanship*, New York: MacMillan Publishing, 1963.
* Rachlis, Eugene, *Horses*, New York: Golden Press, 1965.

Other than drawing upon my own misadventures, misconceptions, and downright stupidity growing up wild and free in the mountain man tradition, there are other sources I have used for information on trapping, survival, animal instinct, woodsmanship, and the mountain man/Indian way of life:

* Blevins, Winfred, *Give Your Heart to the Hawks*, New York: Avon Books/Discus, 1982.
* Chansler, Walter S., *Successful Trapping Methods 2nd Edition*, New York: Van Nostrand Reinhold Company, 1968.
* Christ, Henry I., *Myths and Folklore*, New York: Oxford Book Company, 1956.
* Dobie, Frank J., *The Mustangs*, Boston: Little, Brown and Company, 1952.
* Graves, Richard, Bushcraft, *A Serious Guide to Survival and Camping*, New York: Schocken Books, 1975.

- Roe, Frank Gilbert, *The Indian and the Horse*, Norman, Oklahoma: The University of Oklahoma Press, 1968.
- Russell, Osborne, *Journal of a Trapper*, New York: MJF Books, 1955.
- Utley, Robert M., *A Life Wild and Perilous*, New York: Henry Holt and Company, 1997.
- Vestal, Stanley, *Jim Bridger, Mountain Man*, Lincoln, NE: University of Nebraska Press, 1970.
- Welch, James, *Fools Crow*, New York: Penguin Books, 1986.

�֍ **E N D** ✷

# Index

# P

# About the Author

Gary Spina has ventured half way around the world. Along the way, he has wandered with and encountered many of the interesting characters who now people his writing. He has lived among Indians in Montana and amid adventurers in Alaska. In a sometimes vain attempt to keep himself indoors and fed, he's been a police officer, private detective, journalist, newspaper columnist, sports writer, on-the-road salesman, and truck driver among other pursuits. He is a hunter, trapper, and woodsman, a sea kayaker, and canoeist. He was going to try his hand at rodeo bull riding, but for an accident. That day, in a saloon just across from the rodeo, he accidentally drank up his twenty-five dollar entry fee and without it they wouldn't let him ride.

As a tramp and a merchant marine deckhand, he has walked the rough streets of seaport towns and the peaceful sands of South Pacific paradises. Some of the strangest people he's met have become lifelong friends.

Finally, it was a tough old nun in Washington, D.C. who straightened him out long enough for him to teach English in a Catholic school. But eight years there was long enough to earn a modest pension. He headed west to teach Honors English at an Indian High School in Montana. But he never forgot that old nun in Washington with her pretty smile, her wary eye, and her intriguingly dangerous disposition. He had asked her six times to run away with him and marry him, but she turned him down every time. Still sometimes, even now, on a cold night, over a bottle of whiskey, he wonders whether seven would have been his lucky number.